THE PSYCHO-ANALYTICAL PROCESS

Donald Meltzer

Published for
The Harris Meltzer Trust
by

KARNAC

First published in 1967
Reprinted in 1970, 1979, 1990
The Roland Harris Trust Library No 1
Copyright © Donald Meltzer 1967

This edition published in 2008 by
Karnac Books Ltd
118 Finchley Road
London NW3 5HT

British Library Cataloguing in Publication Data

A.C.I.P. for this book is available from the British Library

ISBN-13: 978-1-85575-668-7

Printed in Great Britain by Biddles Ltd., King's Lynn, Norfolk

www.harris-meltzer-trust.org.uk

www.karnacbooks.com

CONTENTS

PAGE

ACKNOWLEDGEMENT   vi

PREFACE   vii

INTRODUCTION   xi

SECTION I

CHAPTER

   I The Gathering of the Transference   1

  II The Sorting of Geographical Confusions   13

 III The Sorting of Zonal Confusions   23

 IV The Threshold of the Depressive Position   32

   V The Weaning Process   44

SECTION II

 VI The Process with Adult Patients   53

 VII The Cycle of the Process in the Individual Session 66

VIII The Analytical Work   78

 IX Psychoanalysis as a Human Activity   92

APPENDICES A—L   96

INDEX   107

ACKNOWLEDGEMENT

I WISH to thank the following friends for their help and advice in the preparation of this work: Mrs. Esther Bick, Miss Betty Joseph, Miss Patti Koock, Dr. Herbert Rosenfeld, Dr. Hanna Segal, Mr. Adrian Stokes, Miss Doreen Weddell.

PREFACE

OVER the past six years, through lectures and seminars, this book has grown to its present form in the milieu of close cooperation in clinical work and research. Most of its form comes from the author but much of its richness from the students and colleagues with whom it has been "worked through". It began shortly before Melanie Klein's death in 1960, as a series of lecture-seminars to Child Psycho-therapists who had been trained at the Tavistock Clinic. In these sessions material was presented selected by therapists who were having supervision with the author. These presentations were preceded by a 20 minute off-the-cuff lecture on the analytical process, and the nosology and prognosis to be illustrated by the case presentation. These lectures were recorded, mimeographed and distributed.

This method was repeated over those six years with different groups: student psycho-therapists, students of child analysis, the analysts and students of the Argentinian Psycho-analytical Society and finally with a research seminar of student and graduate child analysts. It was possible to operate in this way because of a wide supervision experience, from which timely case material could be drawn. It has been through the abundance of supervision of child and adult cases juxtaposed to the work with my own patients that awareness of the patterns described in the book arose. Publication has come as the logical step after conviction.

I mention these facts to locate the experience here embodied within the framework of psycho-analytical history, to show that a group is at work expanding the theory and practice of developments begun by Melanie Klein. Consequently this book cannot be fruitfully read without reference to this historical context, a minimum requirement being Hanna

Segal's *Introduction to the Work of Melanie Klein*.* It is difficult to imagine that the present book could on the other hand have significance for anyone who has not experienced the analytical process at first hand as a patient. It is intended for the use of practising analysts and as a contribution to a new and widespread interest in the analytical process.

With regard to terminology, most technical terms employed are well known in the Kleinian literature, such as splitting, splitting-and-idealisation, projective identification, internal objects, etc. But others will be less familiar, although they have become common parlance amongst Kleinian analysts. They are largely notational, a style of reference, rather than technical. Their meaning does not involve any increment to theory, but is evident from their context. I refer to such terms as "toilet-breast", "toilet-mummy", "feeding-breast", "little-boy part (of the self)", etc. It is a shorthand for structural reference and its general principles are simple: (1) adult or infantile names are given to objects as they refer to the experience of adult or infantile levels of the personality—cf.— "Mother" or "Mummy"; (2) objects are named as indication of part- or whole-object status—cf.—"Mummy" or "breast"; (3) parts of the self are named to distinguish their level of maturity and leading quality, so as to define the degree of splitting—cf.—the "man", the "little-boy-part", the "baby-penis".

A similar notation indicates the geographical distribution in phantasy, where "internal" and "external" are used to describe inner and outer worlds, while "inside" and "outside" are used to define the relationship to the inside or outside of the body of an object.

Hyphenation is copiously employed in this notation and can always be taken to imply a degree of confusion where terms of the same grammatical value are linked, as in the example of "baby penis-tongue". Thus one would use the term "anus-vagina" rather than a biological term like "cloaca", because the first can be turned round into "vagina-anus" when reproductive functions are being ascribed to the rectum, rather than excretory functions to the uterus (as in infantile concepts of menstruation).

* Published by William Heinemann Medical Books Ltd., London.

However, it has not been possible to write this book without at times transcending in theoretical reference the published literature to date. Some of this is due to contact with colleagues who have not yet published their findings. Where it is my own publication that is lagging behind the text, I have tried to remedy the situation by means of a theoretical appendix to which the reader is referred. This seemed preferable to breaking up the text with footnotes and the reader is advised to leave the appendix to the last, unless he finds the text incomprehensible without reference to it.

One word more by way of preface, namely about the method of exposition. Many colleagues and students have generously written up clinical material for me over the years, intending it for use in this work. However, I have decided in this initial presentation to employ very few clinical examples in the description of the analytic process (Section I), and instead to attempt a generic description of clinical phenomena that would have a vivid reference to the transactions of the consulting room and playroom. This method is intended to evoke in the reader associations to his own experience as patient and analyst. In Section II, which deals with the analyst's task and functions, clinical material will be used which also will illustrate aspects of Section I.

D.M.

INTRODUCTION

THE "doing" of analytical work and the "talking" about it
are very different functions of analysis. The analyst at work
must be "lost" in the analytical process as the musician at his
instrument, relying on the virtuosity of his mind in the depths.
From this absorption he must "surface", between patients, in
repose, in conversation with colleagues and in writing. There
can be little doubt that these two areas of function must
interact if the individual analyst, and psycho-analysis as a
whole, is to develop. Nothing could be more dangerous to
this development than a split between the "doing" and the
"talking", between the practitioner and the theorist.

One safeguard against splitting is the use of language to
bridge and hold together functions and areas of the personality
which have a tendency to recede from one another. It is a
special virtue of Melanie Klein's work that the language
spoken to her patients and to her colleagues was the same,
with a few notable exceptions. Terms such as "paranoid-
schizoid position" and "depressive position" may be necessary
as belonging to a meta-language, to use Bertrand Russell's
term, a "level of abstraction" above the clinical work. But
"projective identification" may have to be changed eventually
to something, perhaps, like "intrusive identification" if only
someone could find a word to express a phantasy function so
remote from consciousness, save in fairy tales.

With these few linguistic exceptions, the language of this
book reflects a basic attitude about the structure of the mind
on the one hand and the nature of the analytical process on
the other, namely that the second is the natural product of
the first. More accurately one might say that the value of
the analytical process derives from the degree to which it is
determined by the structure of the mind. The link is of
course the "transference" and the "counter-transference",

unconscious and infantile functions of the minds of patient and analyst. If the latter's only claim to special qualification is his capacity to deploy his "organ of consciousness" inward to comprehend his counter-transference, the rest of analytical "work" is technical in the session and intellectual in repose. With his technical and intellectual equipment, the analyst undertakes to perform in a special way, and to encourage his patient toward a similar performance, namely to utilise consciousness (of the derivatives of unconscious processes) for the purpose of verbal thought, as distinct from action. This amounts to an undertaking to "contain" the infantile aspects of the mind and only to communicate *about* them. This communication is the analyst's interpretive activity which will, in time, contribute to the patient's capacity for "insight".

But however important interpretation may be to the "cure" and the "insight", it is not the main work of the analyst as regards the establishment and maintenance of the analytical process. This is done by the *creation* of the "setting" in which the transference processes of the patient's mind may discover expression. The word "creation" stresses the nature of this technical part of the work, for it seems clear that a constant process of *discovery* by the analyst is required, referable to the modulation of anxiety on the one hand and the minimising of interference on the other.

Note that the term "modulation" of anxiety has been used rather than "modification", since the latter is surely a function of the *interpretive* aspect of the work while the modulation is managed as part of the *setting*. This modulation· occurs through the patient's repeated experience in analysis that there is a place where the expression of his transference processes will not be met by *counter-transference activity* but only by *analytical activity*, namely a *search for the truth*.

In order for this search for the truth about the patient's mind to proceed, it is necessary that the setting should minimise those interferences with the unfolding and elaboration of his transference such as would be caused by the intrusion of external realities upon the setting. Common sense would predict that this was impossible as regards the age, sex, appearance and character of the analyst. But fortunately analysis is not bound by common sense and finds that the pressure from within the patient toward a resolution for his conflicts will act aside all these external realities if they are not too forcibly obtruded upon him. The secret is stability, and the key to stability is simplicity. Every analyst must work out for himself a simple *style* of analytical work, in time arrangements, financial agreement, room, clothing, modes of expression, demeanour. He must work well within the limits of his physical capacity and his mental tolerance. But also, in the process of discovery with a patient, he must find through his sensitivity the means of modulation required by that individual within the framework of his technique. In a word, he must *preside* over the setting in a way which permits the evolution of the patient's transference.

It can be seen that this view of the analytical process rests primarily on the structural component of metapsychology and, with children as well as adults, envisages both horizontal (age-level) as well as vertical (anatomical and functional) splitting of the self to exist.* And so, to a greater or lesser degree, there is always in existence, if not always available for contact, a most-mature-level of the mind, which, because of its introjective identification with adult internal objects, may reasonably be termed the "adult part". It is this part of the personality with which an alliance is sought and fostered during analytical work. One aspect of analytical work which fosters this alliance involves the indication and explanation of the cooperation required, as well as its encouragement. The hope of the analyst is that this "adult part" will gain increasing control over the "organ of consciousness", and thus of behaviour, not only for the purpose of increasing cooperation but eventually for the development of a capacity for self-analysis.

Consequently a distinction can be drawn between the patient's "analysis", as a potentially life-long process, a way of life of responsibility through insight, and "being analysed" as the method of setting self-analysis in motion. This latter state gives substance to a concept of "termination" as distinct from "interruption" of analysis, and to aims of achievement of basic *organisation* of the personality rather than to the

* *See* Appendix K.

resolution of particular psycho-pathological traits or symptoms. This view is, one might say, a step away from the medical model of psycho-analytic work, an abandonment of concepts such as "illness" and "cure", in favour of a purely meta-psychological view.

It was a natural development that linked psycho-analysis so closely to the medical field and the speciality of neuro-psychiatry; much mutual benefit resulted especially in earlier days when the therapeutic range of analysis was so narrow that differential psychiatric diagnosis served as an essential safeguard to analytic practice. But as psychiatry has moved forward with drugs, psycho-therapies, group treatments and sociological approaches, the pressure upon the psycho-analyst to "cure" the ill has lessened and his position in the world has begun to clarify. Psycho-analysis has become on the one hand the most fruitful method of research into human *mentality* where the concept of "mind" is distinguished from that of "brain", its chief focus. On the other hand psycho-analysis has proved a valuable training-ground and source of information for related fields of psychology, social science and medicine.

Freed of the burden to "cure", psycho-analysis has clearly turned its attention to character development, attracting a different type of patient with different aims. Embracing an area somewhere in the triangle between psychological medicine, education and child-rearing, it seems ready to develop a nosology, prognostic system and method of evaluation of progress separate from the clinical descriptive method used by psychiatry. Its alternative must be a system based on the analytic process as a unified concept, but this cannot be achieved without unity of clinical method. Fortunately it turns out that "clinical method" does not need to include the area of theory and its outcome, interpretation. There is ample scope for unity of clinical experiences to make scientific communication possible as long as the technical aspect of the method is held constant, namely the setting. It is assumed here that any method which does not focus its inquiry on the transference is simply not related to psycho-analysis at all.

A little consideration will quickly reveal how reasonable it is, from the view-point expressed here, that the analysis of children should reveal the analytical process in its purest form. Not only does the child come to analysis innocent of cultural misapprehensions as to the nature of the process, but he takes to it unselfconsciously and without conscious motivation. Since the levels of his mind are poorly differentiated and his life is filled with transference phenomena, the analytical process takes him into its realm unawares. For this paradoxical reason cooperation in analysis cannot be said to develop in children for a very long time. And so it is not reasonable to speak of their being uncooperative either, until a clear alliance has been developed in the "adult" part of their personality, so that its fluctuations in effort can be studied.

For these reasons this book has been constructed around the process as it is revealed in the playroom, and may appear to be germane primarily to the experience of child analysts. However, if readers who lack this area of experience will persevere to Chapter VI, they will find the whole panorama brought into relation with the realities of the adult consulting room. Indeed every analyst is constantly seeing the child, or, more accurately, the various child-parts, of his adult patient in dreams, as well as in the acting-in and acting-out of the transference. Nevertheless it is true that, since an experience of children enriches the work of analysts, so an absence of this experience may render the descriptions of Chapters I–V less vivid.

To return for a moment to the necessity, in the future, of constructing a purely psycho-analytical nosology and method of prognosis. Suggestions toward such a foundation have been indicated along the way in the text for the sake of clinical anchorage. But to be of scientific value, a system of nomenclature and prognosis would have to stand in intimate connection on the one hand with a method of evaluation, and on the other with a clarified and unified concept of the analytical process. Clearly the steps must be: first, analytical process; second, method of evaluation; third, construction of a nosology and prognosis. There can be little doubt that the background work in theory and technique is already in hand, thanks to the genius of a few. It is now feasible for other workers to make their contribution in welding psycho-analysis into a self-contained science, vigorous enough to satisfy its most demanding friends and to fend off its most virulent enemies.

As we are now to trace the evolution of the transference as a process with a natural history of its own, it would perhaps be best from the outset to be clear about the utility on the one hand and the dangers on the other of such a conceptualisation. I have said that an analyst must be "lost" in the inner experience of his patient's material, trusting to his analytic virtuosity in the session to carry on both the technical management and interpretive work. But he must "surface" in repose to understand what he has in fact been doing and what area the analytic process has traversed. From these considerations he may predict its future course and carry on the validation by prediction which is the chief scientific tool of psycho-analysis.

It goes without saying that conviction about analytic theory can only come from experience; each analyst, guided by teachers and the literature, must "discover" the whole of analysis for himself. This is not so in other sciences, I believe, where absolute interdependence of each area of theory does not exist. If they are pyramids which stand upon their bases, psycho-analysis is one which stands on its apex, the concept of the unconscious. Its history resembles the game of building with match-sticks on the top of a bottle, and such is the structure of theories which take shape in the analyst's mind as he develops. As with the builder-on-the-bottle, this structure is in constant danger from every disturbance, particularly attacks from his own infantile structures. Until the analyst's experience is wide on the one hand and his character has been stabilised by analytic treatment on the other, this structure of theory is continually toppling down under the stress of analytic work, its pain, confusion, worry, guilt, disappointment. The "surfacing" to take stock, which occurs while the student is in analysis and while the young analyst is having supervision, must eventually be taken over as an autonomous process. To this function the conceptualisation of the analytic process can make a contribution—and thereby to the research capacity of the developing analyst. By this I mean his capacity to "discover" psycho-analytic phenomena beyond the verification of all he has been taught.

If this is the value of the conception, we must remember its dangers, namely the temptation to guard ourselves against the distresses enumerated above by scotomisation, by obsessional control, by docile dependence on and acquiescence in theory. And so I mention again, before we start, the Chapters to follow cannot be "used" in the consulting room, but only in repose, while writing notes, reviewing progress, presenting material, writing papers.

CHAPTER I

THE GATHERING OF THE TRANSFERENCE

CHILDREN approach analysis, as they do any new experience in life, under the guidance and authority of their parents. It has been the custom to think that the wish to please parents, the hope for gratification of secret yearnings, and the expectation of relief for current distress were mingled in varying degrees to propel them toward the new experience, while anxieties held them back. Alternatively one might think that the motivational pattern is more completely unconscious and belongs to a general category of the wish to maintain the status quo versus the drive toward integration. I do not think that these two points of view are by any means incompatible but I find the latter more in keeping with my experience and my way of describing analytic phenomena.

From this view-point a child's life at the inception of analysis would appear to be full to overflowing with objects in the outside world—parents, siblings, relatives, servants, teachers, pets, toys, machines and nature generally. While his tendency, impelled by various drives and anxieties, is to extend the boundaries of self and to engulf every new object, he also suffers from a fear of overextension—of "getting lost" in fact, and for this reason attempts to maintain a defined perimeter. The geography of this perimeter, as regards the outside world, is primarily, as in so many games, defined as the emotional distance from "home", which is the domicile, truly, but of course fundamentally the bodies of his parents, especially mother. Thus persons and things possess a valence of positive and negative as they are felt to be friendly to the parents, the intensity of the valence varying with the degree of intimacy, friendly or hostile. It is for this reason that a phobia, for instance, will almost always be found to have a link with a parental phobic trend. On the other hand we know that an oedipal negative valence arises the moment a too-positive intimacy with a parental figure is suspected.

I think we can safely say that children "size up" their analyst in this way, one eye on the parent, one on the analyst, watching their interaction, in the moments of meeting. We may conceive of the children's inability very usefully to separate in these terms, as due not primarily to a persecutory outcrop but because of their inability to internalise the juxta-position of parental figure and analyst for the purpose of "sizing up". A child who has more capacity for introjection can do it, utilising data derived from a parent relative to the analyst, and vice versa, in isolation one from the other. The way the parents have presented the need and purpose of analysis, for instance, can be juxtaposed in thought to the analyst's presentation, or attitude, or manner. Any dis-harmony has the effect of a negative valence accruing to the analytic procedure or to the analyst as a person. For this reason the careful coaching of the parents for the preparation of the child for his first session and for the handling of the child in various eventualities arising out of that session, is well worth the time, despite the fact that one often finds that the most careful instruction is lost in the heat of the moment.

This way of understanding the problem at hand, in the general sense of introducing a new person into a child's life, would suggest that the narrow gap between friendliness and persecutory or oedipal negative valence must be utilised by the correct degree of friendly but not too intimate relation between parent and stranger being made evident to the child. This is in fact what the instructed teacher or doctor will do by demeanour, mode of address, a brief chat with parent before turning attention to the child with a degree of physical as well as emotional contact.

But the requirements of the analytic process do not really seem likely to be fulfilled in the long run with this sort of beginning, since our aims are very different from those of the new teacher or doctor. We do not seek to establish a relation of trust and obedience to ourselves as parental surrogates in a limited area. We wish to undertake a new and far-reaching relation which can be set apart from the child's life at home and develop into a *private, cooperative, responsible work* eventually. This fourfold alliance to the child's most mature aspects can only, I believe, be achieved by the methods set out by Melanie Klein in which interpretation, coupled with clarification of the setting and the method of analysis, is utilised to set going the analytic process, with all its organic qualities which we propose to investigate—its "natural history", as I have called it.

It would therefore seem best, with this aim in view, that the parents should tell the child as little as possible about the reasons for bringing it to analysis or the aims of the process, but only *information* regarding time, frequency, name of the analyst, indicating that the rest of the child's questions can be asked of the analyst. Similarly it would seem desirable that the contact between parent and analyst be as minimal and equivocal as politeness will allow.

This procedure is bound to create a tendency toward the most persecutory negative valence in the child in regard to the analyst who must attempt to offset it as quickly as possible through the means of interpreting unconscious and conscious anxieties and by clarification of the setting, method and purpose of the analytic procedure.

What happens as a consequence of this type of approach, the introductory period in the analysis of children, I call the "gathering of the transference processes". It may last a few weeks or it may last several months. I can hardly imagine an intractable resistance to analysis taking shape in this period, granted adequate technique and minimal correctness of interpretation, except for one reason, *folie a deux* between mother and child. I am tempted to say "person bringing the child" but do not really think this is correct, because I have had experience where it was not the mother who was "bringing" but was the mother who was involved in the "folie" which prevented the "gathering" from sufficiently taking shape to set the process of analysis in motion.

We have already cursorily considered the organisation of the child's life-space as regards the general distribution of positive and negative valence and the creation of a perimeter from within which all negative objects, feared and hated alike, tend to be excluded, and within which the processes of object relation and identification are in some degree of flux. What is also in a constant state of flux is his relation to internal objects; instability is the most significant aspect of personality organisation by which the child can be differentiated from the adult, from the psycho-analytical point of view. Not only are his internal relations in a constant flux, but the differentiation of internal and external is constantly blurred by the external-isation of the internal situation and by its being acted out. The objects in the outside world which habitually represent certain aspects of internal reality may have already taken on a sufficient constancy to be worthy of the name of symptom, as in a phobia, an obsessional ritual, a fixed paranoid relation to the neighbourhood bully or food fads. To a certain extent one can speak of the character of a child, but only in extremely ill children does one find the rigidity and limitation which approaches the quality of constancy or crystallisation seen in the adult patient. Such children, in fact, we tend to describe as little old men or women for just this reason of rigidity.

But generally, as I have said, flux in internal relations and fluidity of transition to acting out is the order of the day in children, and it is just this flux and fluidity which are the main facets of their availability to the analytic approach. What I have described could be rephrased as follows: children's most mature level of relations to external objects is constantly contaminated by the uncontrolled acting out of the consequences of the constant flux in the internal and infantile levels of their psychic life. There is no area free from this contamination. However a child's awareness of disturbance varies greatly, being most keen in the young child who is aware of an interference with his wish to fulfil his parents' demands and expectations. When the splitting of levels becomes more constant, as in latency, the incursions from psychic reality are either rationalised as ego syntonic or denied, from the point of view of their significance. Thus the latency child so often feels its parents to be "in a bad mood" or "making a fuss about nothing" in regard to an outbreak of outrageous behaviour on his part. They "take it too seriously" he feels; "all the boys (or girls) do it" or "feel that way" or are freely permitted by their parents to do what he has just been refused.

In a word, the child's life is full of transference processes. So indeed is the adolescent's life (age 11 to X), but with an important difference. Where the child externalises his internal objects in his acting out, the adolescent projects parts of his self and thus enters into a far more narcissistic type of acting out in which collusion plays a great part.* This distinction is of great importance in understanding why children are relatively easy to induct into the analytic process, while adolescents, more like psychotics, are so difficult. Because the children externalise objects and then enter into transference relations to these object-surrogates in the outside world, they perform in a way which is generally alien to their best level of relationship to that person or pet or thing. While the external surrogate may be drawn by provocation into acting the desired role, as laid down in the dream which is being expelled, so to speak, it does so with a degree of in-built resistance. This is most easily seen with toys which, when inappropriately used, break, get lost, prove inadequate to the role imposed on them, etc. Similarly with animals, who quickly "leave the field", as the gestalt writers describe, when excessive demands are made. Only humans, and especially adults, offer, because of their own disturbance or ill-directed goodwill, really suitable object-surrogate capability. For this reason, despite the child's life being "full-up" with objects, any adult with whom he has repeated contact tends to accrue transference significance, as money in the bank accrues interest, simply by virtue of "being there".

Nevertheless, despite disturbance and even great quantities of ill-directed goodwill, most adults in a child's world do not have the requisite intensity of interest to sustain a transference role without an occasional revolt against the tyranny and restriction. For this reason, with the exception of parental willingness to be idealised or of a nanny or grandparent to be supra-parental, the child's transference processes are forced almost constantly to seek new objects. This constitutes a pressure toward retention of the disturbed internal situation and the evolution of symptoms as a consequence. Where a child and an adult form a stable acting out collaboration, the

* *See* Appendix A.

folie a deux, so refractory to analysis, arises. It is, in my experience, rare and generally involves a psychotic adult. The narcissistic type of collusion between children, so prevalent in puberty, has not the same anti-analytic armour-platedness.

This feature, the readiness to co-opt a new, repeatedly encountered adult as a surrogate for internal objects, constitutes the major area of availability of the child to analysis, like the charge on an ion or on unsaturated linkage in an organic compound. Faced with the equivocal quality of both the setting and the person of the analyst, the child's transference needs or tendencies begin to "feel-out" the situation and one *ballon d'essai* after another, at first perhaps slowly, but soon more and more rapidly, begins to appear in play, demeanour, behaviour, verbalisation. These feelers are, we believe, intended to involve the analyst in a mutual acting out and their greeting by interpretation is at first rather shocking to the child. These initial interpretations must be gently couched and amply accompanied by explanations of how analysis differs from ordinary situations at home and school.

What do we think happens when we interpret instead of joining in the acting out of the transference? First of all we find, as Melanie Klein has shown us, that anxiety in deeper levels is relieved. But do we know how or why? W. R. Bion* has suggested that the patient, like the baby, externalises an internal situation by projective identification of a part of the self in distress. This part is subsequently experienced as returned, divested of its pain through the process of understanding. In order to achieve this function it is clear that the analyst must indeed receive the projective identification and its pain without being dominated and driven to action by it. The analyst's attitude, of receptiveness, introjection, self-control and, above all, the desire to understand, cannot be counterfeited. I do not wish to lay too much stress on the accuracy of interpretation, for one may receive projections and understand them long before one is able to verbalise them accurately. But I have no doubt that the exploratory nature of the interpretive process is essential to enable this feeling-out to gather momentum.

* *Learning From Experience*—(Heinemann) 1962.

In the face of this gathering momentum the first week-end strikes like a wolf in the fold and I have never yet seen or heard of a child patient who did not return on the following Monday in a state of inner rage, covered by the "crust", as Freud calls it. These two processes, the relief derived from understanding and the shock of separation set in motion the rhythm which is the wave-form, as it were, of the analytic process, recurring at varying frequencies, session by session, week by week, term by term and year by year.

This tendency for transference processes to find expression where their anxieties can find relief results in the phenomenon which I have called, "gathering of the transference". Where the child takes to analysis well this may happen very rapidly indeed at first, and result in the type of improvement in the clinical disturbance outside analysis which has been called, somewhat misleadingly, "transference cure", a term borrowed from adult analysis where it is probably synonymous with "flight into health". It is important to prepare parents for such an early improvement and to assure them that it will not last, whether or not they would seriously think of removing the child from analysis.

This initial gathering of the transference is more obvious in children than adult patients, in whom the so-called pre-formed transference is so prominent in the early weeks and months. Children, thanks to their relative naivety about psycho-analysis, do not present this facade, either of pseudo-cooperation or pseudo-transference, so the true nature of the events which set an analysis in motion are more clearly revealed by them. In fact the events are really the same for all patients, and while the child will at the beginning try to impose on the analyst the role of some well-known figure such as doctor in the case of a male analyst or teacher in the case of a woman, the adult or adolescent will impose the role of "psycho-analyst" as derived from reading, films, rumour and phantasy. But this initial gambit is of no real consequence and need hardly be dealt with, as it bursts like a bubble pricked by the first interpretation that really strikes to the depths.

Each child soon settles into his own method of presentation of transference phenomena, his own style, as it were. Little children will usually play with the toys, show their anxieties in gross behaviour such as flight from the room, and very ostentatiously either relate to or completely ignore the person of the analyst. Latency children most often will recapitulate their school behaviour, sitting, drawing or writing. The pubertal child may want to talk but be unable to accept the dependence and loss of anchorage to reality on the couch.

All these too, being but matters of style, are of little consequence. The essential process, the evolution of the transference, goes on without ever being visible to the analyst until the setting has been circumscribed and defined so that the anxieties are being contained within it. Again this takes the form, with young children, of the analyst needing to define and impose the geographical limits of the setting. With the latency child the transference passes to the person and behaviour of the analyst, that is, to his refusal to fit in with the role, doctor, teacher, nannie, uncle, or the like, which the child casts for him. With the pubertal child it centres around qualities of a wider social significance such as the analyst's refusal to represent the "adult world" as against the "teenagers".

During the initial weeks, when technical problems of the setting are being dealt with, the material seems to shift and dart about, from the point of view of its latent content, and to be nebulous and equivocal in its quality, genital oedipal one moment, deeply infantile the next, with persecutory and depressive anxieties alternating and confusions emerging from all levels. In a sense the material is both a vehicle for the problems of the setting and a reflection of the phantasies thrown up by the ways in which these problems are handled. Firmness in handling a small child's separation problem in the waiting room may throw up material of projective identification with a persecutor, which requires setting the limits of aggressive behaviour. This might lead to passive feminine oedipal material, which requires clarification of the restriction on body contact: such restriction may bring forth masculine castration anxiety and homosexual seductive placation with sweets from the pocket, say, which would lead to clarification of the analyst's reasons for refusing this or other gifts. An explanation could lead to manic anal expulsive behaviour and the need to defecate, which requires clarification of the analyst's insistence on accompanying the child to the lavatory and the working out of details about the actual help required by the child to undress, dress, clean, flush the toilet, etc., as distinct from his seductiveness on the one hand or persecutory anxiety on the other—and so on.

In other words in these early sessions material tends not to derive its latent content from previous material, as it will ever after in the analysis, but to appear as a response to the *behaviour* of the analyst in relation to the setting. However its tendency to *re*appear subsequently is related to the interpretive process and its capacity to make a link with this configuration of phantasy, to "hook" it, and hold it as a transference pattern in the analysis.

While all of these fleeting patterns of phantasy and potential transference are rising in response to problems of the setting, another sequence has been set in motion in response to the first week-end break, namely a sequence of transference configuration centering around problems of separation and therefore of individuation. All the devices known to the child, of greater and lesser omnipotence, are tried out in turn, discarded, tried again—and eventually abandoned in favour of a more and more consistent use of the only infallible defence against separation, massive projective identification.

This is the essential sequence in the deepening of the transference which sets going the analytic process, with all its autonomous power. But this deepening can falter and long periods be spent at lesser depths and more random analytic work if the technical handling of the sequence of defences against the experience of separation are not adequate. Delaying tactics, last moment destruction and denigration of the setting, stealing, leaving before time (either leaving the consulting room or leaving the contact), manic reversal by going *to* the parent in the waiting room, and countless other devices must be met, analysed for their underlying anxieties and dealt with by tightening of the technique of the setting. Again the form of the problem is different with adult patients, centering more on the problems of time, fees, modes of activity and of communication, but the process is the same.

These two problems, the gathering of the transference configurations that arise in respect of the setting and the deepening of the transference response to the separations, interact with one another to intensify the involvement in the analysis. They mobilise the child's omnipotence in his attempt to stabilise the situation as the struggles against the evolution of dependence of any sort on the analytic process and the person of the analyst. Offset against these attempts by the patient to control the situation are the services of the analyst in regard to those psychic pains, which are being both touched and intensified. His reception of projections of the psychic pain serves as a modulating factor until their modification by interpretation can be effected.

Slowly this relatively haphazard movement of the transference lessens as the setting is erected in its many complex facets and the rhythm of the analytic process asserts itself. Seldom does it really settle before the consequences of a holiday break have been dealt with. It is perhaps the only phase of analysis where experience counts greatly in relation to time. The tempo of this first phase is determined to a considerable degree by the technical skill and clinical judgement of the analyst, unlike the later phases where the working-through goes on largely at its own pace, determined by the patient's structure and constitution. This point will be clarified in the subsequent Chapters of this section.

In these Chapters on the "natural history" of the analytic process (Chapters I–V) the clinical emphasis will be, for reasons explained in the Introduction, on the process as seen in the analysis of children, leaving the orientation of the whole to adult analysis for Chapter VI. But some attention might well be paid here to the apparent differences in the approach and induction period from the adult non-psychotic patient, in order to demonstrate that these striking differences are in fact superficial, differences in form rather than in structure.

The adult comes to analysis with his character more crystallised and his patterns of transference to external objects more stable than the child. But very widespread contamination of his adult life exists nonetheless. His sexual life is highly contaminated with infantile sexuality so that his spouse is also his delinquent sibling, as a continuation of the patterns of adolescence. His children contain infant parts of himself in projection, to whom he acts either as the idealising or per-secuting parent. His most infantile persecutors may now live on Mars or in Russia but they exist, and his attitude to money, possessions, social status, politics and even his field of special skill and knowledge is bound to be more or less contaminated with infantile significance. In the structural sense it seems certain that most adults continue to have an adolescent personality structure until what Elliott Jaques has called the "mid-life crisis", when either a struggle toward greater integration (and with it a rebellion against their cultural patterns) commences or a return to latency period rigidity ensues, the "settling down into middle age".

Whether the adult patient comes to analysis during this prolonged adolescence or in the throes of mid-life crisis or in the latency period morass of middle age, his containment of infantile structures and his acknowledgement of psychic reality are bound to be severely limited.

The adult's personality structures, then, from the psycho-pathological point of view, differs little from that of the child. In regard to motivation the situation is similar, the difference again being more apparent than real. What analyst can look back on his motives for entering analysis without realising that "dumb luck" and not astuteness of judgement brought him to the couch. It is so with all patients for no person who has not experienced the analytic process can really comprehend its emotional meaning, regardless of his intellectual grasp of the literature. We were beggars when we thought we were patrons, patients when we thought ourselves students.

As spurious as is the motivation of adults, so equally false is their vaunted cooperation. With all sincerity, consciously, and with every effort of intellect, they cannot follow the primary rule, so often wrongly apprehended as "to say every-thing that comes to your mind". In reality we wish our patients to "observe their mental states and communicate their observa-tions", which they cannot do, and will not be able to do with any accuracy or consistency for some years. They can neither "observe", so constricted is their consciousness in relation to internal processes, nor can they "communicate", so inadequate is their vocabulary, developed in relation to objects and events of the outside world.

In fact, as with the child, the adult patient is bound, for a long period, to "act in the transference" to a very great extent—and, sadly for family and friends, to act out as well. Like the child patient, therefore, the inception of treatment with an adult patient also really commences after the first week-end break. Similar to the child's a period of general improvement accompanies the "gathering of the transference" and is then disrupted by the commencement of patterns of acting out, as the main stream of transference takes shape, and the "natural history of the analytic process" takes on a life of its own.

If all this applies to the adult patient who seeks analysis himself, out of insight and knowledge, how much more does it apply to the great majority of patients who come, like children, at the behest of doctors, spouses and friends, expecting to be "cured" through submission to "being analysed"

CHAPTER II

THE SORTING OF GEOGRAPHICAL CONFUSIONS

In the first Chapter I have described my experience of the initial phase of the analytic process with children, carrying as a central thesis the contention that this process has a natural history of its own, determined by the structure of the mental apparatus at deeply unconscious levels. If this process is adequately presided over by the analyst through the creation of an adequate setting and through an interpretive intervention sufficiently correct and timely to modify the severest anxieties and facilitate working-through, a sequence of phases can be seen (in retrospect mainly) to have emerged, the second of which I wish now to illustrate.

The first week-end separation sets in train a modality of relationship at deep levels of the unconscious which is increased in intensity as the infantile transference processes are gathered and brought to bear in the analysis. This modality, or the trend toward it, is released by every regular separation experience and, later in analysis, will be revived by every *un*planned break in the analytic continuity. The modality to which I refer is the infantile tendency to massive projective identification with external, and soon also with internal, objects. It arises from a configuration of motives and gives rise to a spectrum of consequences which need detailed examination. First, however, a general economic principle should be clarified. The duration of the phase dominated by any particular transference organisation is not really predictable at present, as the factors governing mobility of defences, the intensity of the drive toward integration, the capacity to accept dependence, etc., are all at present obscure and are ordinarily put together under the rubric of "constitutional", which, whatever its biological reference, in practice probably means that we can only assess them in retrospect but not in prospect. In the second place, the term "dominate the transference" must also be taken as a relative one, since the economics of that disposition is obscure. The analytic process is a cyclical one, and the phases which I trace here in a panoramic way can to some degree be seen to appear in sequence in every session, every week, every term, every year—that is, in all four of the cyclical time units of the analytic process. The phase under discussion, being concerned with the experience of separation and of separate identity, naturally tends more to dominate the beginning and end of such cycles—session, week, term, year. But one can reasonably say that the analysis itself is being "dominated" by this dynamism as long as it occupies an overwhelming portion of the analytic time and until the anxieties with which it is concerned have been elucidated so that the working-through can commence. It is probably a correct view that this working-through never completely ceases, which is only another way of saying that the struggle against regression and disintegration is continual.

Turning now to the various motives underlying the tendency to massive projective identification, the major ones could be briefly listed as follows: intolerance of separation; omnipotent control; envy; jealousy; deficiency of trust; excessive persecutory anxiety. These can immediately be seen to overlap —or rather to interlock.

(1) Intolerance to separation can be said to exist when there is present an absolute dependence on an external object in order to maintain integration. This can be seen in autistic and schizophrenic children in whom the need for physical contact, or constant attention, or to be held in contact by constant verbalisation, reveals the absence of the psychic equivalent of the skin.* They require an external object to hold together the parts of the self so as to form an area of life space inside the self which can contain the objects of psychic reality.

(2) Where the differentiation between good and bad is poorly defined due to inadequate or faulty splitting-and-idealisation of self and objects, the use of projective identification

* *See* Appendix B.

for the purposes of omnipotent control can be seen to operate as a precondition for an object relation, in preference to narcissistic organisation. This is evident in very paranoid structure (*see* Betty Joseph's paper "Persecutory Anxiety in a four year old Boy", *Int. J. Psycho-Anal.*, Vol. XLVII).

(3) The role of envy we need not devote much time to as it has been so richly explored by Melanie Klein in *Envy and Gratitude* and *On Identification*.

(4) Jealousy is a complicated emotion and its differentiation from envy can often be somewhat more complicated than 2-body or 3-body formulation suggested by Melanie Klein. This difficulty comes from two directions: there is a primitive elaboration of envy of the mother or the father or of their coital relationship which is so oral, so part-object and so sanctimonious in its application that I have called it "delusional jealousy"* (even though this comes dangerously close to the term "delusions of jealousy" used in the psychiatric literature on paranoia, etc.). This jealousy is delusional because it is based on an *omniscient* relation to the mother's body which envisages internal babies disporting themselves in every conceivable way, especially those ways most longed for and frustrated in the infantile organisation. It is not actually jealousy because it is in fact a devious representation of an envious attitude toward the adult figures.

In the second place there is possessive-jealousy which would appear to be a primitive, highly oral and part-object form of love. It is 2-body and yet is not really envy; it might seem to be included in Melanie Klein's description of envy-of-the-breast-that-feeds-itself. It is seen with extraordinary intensity in the autistic children and in children whose drive to maturity is very low, so that they wish either to remain infantile or to die. This means in their unconscious to return-to-sleep-inside-mother. It is this primitive form of possessive jealousy which plays an important role in perpetuating massive projective identification of this peculiar withdrawn, sleepy sort.

(5) Deficiency of trust is more doubtful as -a factor at this phase, since it is generally a consequence of excessively destructive projection. But I think it can be isolated in a particular form related to secretiveness or trickiness. Where

* *See* Appendix C.

3

the mode of entry in projective identification is accomplished, in phantasy, by a deception or ruse, rather than by violence, distrust of the object, and consequent claustrophobia is intense, since the object is suspected of super-trickiness in its apparent vulnerability. This seems to me to be a distinctive phenomenon which cannot be attributed to parental inconsistency or deception since it appears in analysis as a positive preference for a cloak-and-dagger world. It plays an important role in paranoia and in the perverse attitude generally.

(6) Finally we come to the factor of excessive persecutory anxiety. Here I would think we are now in a position to make a qualitative distinction to enlarge on the general quantitative principle laid down by Melanie Klein, with special reference to what W. R. Bion has called "nameless dread",* and I have described as "terror".† In both cases, paranoid anxieties which are fundamentally unbearable in quality have been described, as distinguished from other forms of persecution which may rise to an intensity which is unbearable in quantity.

Before outlining the consequences of this massive attack on the individuality of objects, and of the analyst in the transference, it is useful to attempt to catalogue briefly some of the typical behavioural manifestations seen in the playroom. A tenable classification might be as follows: (*a*) utilisation of the body of the analyst as a part of the self; (*b*) utilisation of the room as the inside of an object; in such situations the analyst tends to represent a part-object inside this object, while being also equated with the object; (*c*) reversal of the adult-child relationship; where the analyst is made to contain and represent an alienated part of the infantile self; (*d*) exertion of omnipotent control over the analyst.

(*a*) It is more characteristic of younger children and of autistic and very psychotic children to make a frontal approach to the body of the analyst. Here technique plays a large part in determining either its perseverance or its mutation into forms employing somewhat more symbol formation. Probably the autistic children are the most persistent in this matter, despite technical attempts to divert it, and a case may perhaps

* *Learning From Experience*—(Heinemann) 1962.
† *See* Appendix C.

be made for its toleration temporarily if the child is clearly driven by anxiety about fragmentation.* Climbing on the lap, looking into eyes, ears and mouth, concrete representations of eating the analyst's words, pushing the head into the analyst's abdomen, encircling the body by the analyst's arms, pushing the genital or bottom against the analyst—these are some typical modes of approach. When yielded to, an almost immediate manic sweep follows and a shift of material can be seen. An autistic boy will rush to the window and gesture in triumph toward the birds in the garden, though they are usually the objects of enraged fist-shaking when he feels that he is outside and the garden is experienced as the inside of the mother's body. After hearing a dog bark in the garden, a little boy leaned against me briefly, then made a dive behind the couch and barked excitedly.

These types of contact may result in a state of massive projective identification, the physical contact providing an experience of a portal of entry. I mention this at some length to distinguish it as a general problem connected with projective identification, from attitudes and behaviour toward the analyst's body which are *manifestations of an existing state* of projective identification. An autistic child in such an existing state will take the analyst's hand to use it as a tool to open a door or cut a piece of paper. A paranoid child may scheme to get or demand to wear the analyst's glasses in order to see more clearly or try to use his pen, convinced that he could write or draw if he had it.

(*b*) Utilisation of the room as the inside of an object is often made clear by the very mode of entry into the room, in a rush, or knocking against the door jamb, or by a mode of looking about as if in a vast arena. Conversely the phantasy of having remained sequestered inside the analyst during a separation may be expressed by hiding behind the door in the waiting room or under a chair. Looking out of the window, even on to a bare brick wall, as in my own playroom, can become a significant mode of activity, and throwing objects out of the door or window may figure as a way of representing the expulsion of rivals or persecutors. Confusion about time can often be noted as an accompanying phenomenon so that

* *See* Appendix B.

claustrophobic anxiety may be expressed by a suspicious monitoring of the analyst's watch. The intense erotisation of the situation is often manifest and may express itself by complaints about the room being hot or by intense sensitivity to, and curiosity about, sounds from other areas of the house. The walls of the room often seem highly erotised, are felt and stroked, or conversely may be objects of sadistic inquiry by burrowing, investigating the entry and exit of pipes, wires, the structure of doors and windows and the origins of structural or decorative defects.

The relation to the analyst at such times is peculiar and mixed. Less psychotic children will maintain a running commentary with the analyst, while dramatising their phantasies of entry, possession, entrapment, persecution, etc. More psychotic or younger children are more likely to become lost in the phantasy and ignore the analyst as a person, so that the analyst feels, in his interpretive work, as if he were an outside observer and commentator. At other times he may figure as a part-object-inside-the-mother, usually the father's penis or an inside-baby, in either case persecutory, even if highly erotic in significance. It is at such times, in my experience, that the most unexpected explosions of anxiety may occur and, in keeping with this, outbreaks of unusually dangerous aggression. For some reason, probably connected with the phantasy of intrusion and the fear of being spied out, the analyst's eyes seem to be a particular object of attack. But even more dangerous is the sudden identification with the persecutor which may terminate anxiety attacks, resulting in vicious and uncompromising assault.

(*c*) Reversal of the adult-child-relation may be the most prominent representation of massive projective identification and must, like the exerting of omnipotent control, be carefully distinguished from role playing as a mode of communication. It is seen particularly in children starting school, in school-phobics, or their converse, in the child who assaults other children at school. I find that children who have split-off and projected valuable and constructive parts of the self ("mutilations of the ego")* and are functioning at a defective level with much despair about maturation and learning—that

* *See* Appendix D.

these children also become tyrannical teachers or irritable mothers for very long and discouraging periods of analysis. The analyst in such cases is not really requested to act a role but is treated *as* a child, often one among many imaginary children in the playroom.

(*d*) This process of reversal shades subtly into the process of exerting omnipotent control over the analyst. Every conceivable technique is involved, verbal and non-verbal, ranging from coercion, threats, seduction, blackmail, pretended helplessness, feigned crying, exacting promises—all of which can be summed up by one concept, an attempt to induce the analyst to commit a breach of technique. The fact that the omnipotent control is exerted through the phantasy of projective identification is not immediately evident but is seen in the consequences of a breach of technique forced by one of the above methods. The material may suddenly shift to inside-the-object modes already mentioned with evident claustrophobic anxieties. Or an immediate manic response with delayed hypochondriacal consequences may be the result. In a more psychotic patient an immediate shift of most striking type can take place with analyst-like behaviour, making interpretations, commencing a lecture or scolding of a contemptuous sort. On the other hand a sudden regression may be seen, with infantile posturing, finger sucking, going to sleep. Most confounding perhaps is an acute anxiety attack with rushing from the room and refusal to return, in which case prompt recognition and interpretation of the technical breach and of the concrete experience of omnipotent entry and control are required.

It must be understood that the term "breach of technique" is one which refers to the particular analyst's established modes for managing the setting. Early in analysis, when activities requiring technical handling are likely to be at their height, these modes have seldom been elaborated in detail. Certainly I for one am in favour of a gradual working out of such modes with each individual child, starting with a rather loose technique which can be tightened as indicated by events particularly of the types described under headings (*a*) and (*d*) ("utilisation of the analyst's body" and "exerting of omnipotent control"). By this means, imposing restrictions on the basis of clear instances of untoward consequences in the analysis, frees the process from qualities of rigidity which always appear as arbitrary and basically hostile in the child's eyes.

Having now to some extent explored the motives for the massive projective identification which blurs the boundaries of self and object in the transference and produces attendant geographical confusion, and having described some of the typical forms of behaviour by which it is manifest in the analytic session, we are free to turn to a more general consideration of the analytic process as a whole and the role played in it by this phase. I have tried in the earlier sections to make clear that the basic problem is one of psychic pain and the need for an object in the outside world that can contain the projection of it—in a word, what I have come to call the "toilet-breast". By this name I mean to convey both the part-object nature of the relationship and the quality of being valued and needed, but not loved. This I think is very important to recognise in order to understand the inevitable dearth of depressive anxieties in this phase. That is not to say that depressive anxieties are not emerging during this period of the analysis in relation to all sorts of other transference aspects, but the central transactions which I have outlined that are referable to the geographical confusions, have little depressive anxiety attending them.

The splitting, rather, of the object in a severe way takes place and may persevere for a long time, so that the analyst is in effect *only* a toilet and all good things for introjection come from mother, teacher, siblings, friends. This does not mean that an introjective process does not in fact take place, but that it is not acknowledged in the analysis: it is rather, attributed, and indeed experienced, elsewhere. Thus a child may for a long time bring toys, sweets, food or books from home, do homework or knit. The reason for the rigidity of this splitting is clearly to be seen when the split begins to break down and the severe anxieties of soiling, polluting and poisoning the feeding breast become so clear. This is rather beautifully illustrated in "The Narrative" in later sessions when the threat of termination brings it forth with desperate urgency.

This split in the transference amounts to a type of denial of psychic reality and much acting out at home in relation to food may accompany it. Thus it becomes clear that the geographical confusion at this time involves not only a confusion between the inside and outside of the object but also a confusion between external reality and psychic reality. Only with the establishment of the toilet-breast as an object in psychic reality through the repeated experience of it externally in the transference, is the relinquishment of massive projective identification possible, since this mechanism aims at escaping from an unbearable infantile identity. Once this separate identity has thus been made bearable through the modulation of pain, the way is opened for other developmental steps, as I shall discuss in the chapters on subsequent phases in the analytic process.

It is in this phase that we can most graphically see the truth of the great discovery by Melanie Klein, amplified in recent writings by W. R. Bion, that the most primitive form of relief of psychic pain is accomplished by the evacuation into the external object of parts of the self in distress and the persecutory debris of attacked internal objects, receiving back through the introjective aspect the restored objects and relieved parts of the self. In its most concrete form with children actual urination and defecation, using the toilet or, unfortunately on occasions, the consulting room takes place. Most striking is the change in the demeanour of the child at start and finish of such sessions, the relief mixed with contempt with which, without a goodbye, he cheerfully leaves, in contrast with the frantic and disorganised bursting-in type of entry.

I have called this object in the transference the "toilet-breast" because this is its most primitive representation prior to the defence, by horizontal splitting of the mother, which locates the toilet functions below, in connection with her buttocks, while reserving the feeding function for the upper part of the mother's body, breasts, nipples, eyes and mouth—and therefore her mind.

In adult patients the phenomena are more subtle, some of which I have described as the phenomenology of the "pseudo-mature" aspect of the personality, seen in so many cases of border-line or more severe psycho-pathology, in my paper on "Anal Masturbation and Its relation to Projective Identification".*

* *Int. J. of Psycho-Analysis.* Vol 47. Parts 2—3.

I stress the relation of this phase of geographical confusion of the analytic process particularly to adult cases of borderline or more severe psychopathology since the resolution of this configuration of object relation stands as the border between mental illness (psychosis) and mental health, just as the resolution of the obstacles to the dependent introjective relation to the breast traverses the border between mental instability and mental stability, and as the passing of the oedipus complex leads from inmaturity to maturity.* It is a phase of analysis which can last for years with very disturbed patients and, in my experience, may not be very satisfactorily resolved at all and prove an intractable resistance where inadequate environmental support renders the analytic breaks intolerable, in children as well as adults. However, while almost endless patience may be required of the analyst in this phase—and tolerance—progress is almost always steadily achieved. The patient who cannot manage it will either break down at a holiday or leave before or after one. This situation, therefore, is one to which the analytic method seems basically adequate and should be distinguished from those we will meet later which more correctly deserve the name of intractable resistances. In other words, if an analyst can bear to persevere when geographical confusions are in the forefront of the transference he will certainly be rewarded with progress, no matter how slow, for this progress is in almost no way dependent on the cooperation of the adult part of the personality. A striking example of this is seen with disturbed adolescents whose primary mode of effecting projective identification may be to miss sessions for prolonged periods or to miss a percentage of each week's sessions. The analyst who can hold on, while managing the technical problems so as not to seem to compound the delinquency toward the parents, will succeed.

As the dominance of geographical confusion recedes from the transference, the mid-week begins to clear and to be dominated in turn by the configuration to which we must now turn attention. But for a very long time in the analysis this pattern of massive projective identification must be expected in the region of every break, especially those outside the analytic routine.

* *See* Appendix E.

CHAPTER III

THE SORTING OF ZONAL CONFUSIONS

In the first two Chapters I have traced the early phases of the analytic process, first the gathering of the transference processes into the treatment, and second the differentiation of self and object which is brought about by the systematic investigation of the operation of massive projective identification, as it is intensified in the transference in relation to separation. It seems clear that, since massive projective identification can function to counter any configuration producing psychic pain at infantile levels, no other problem can really be worked through until this mechanism has been to some considerable degree abandoned. In the neurotic patient this may be accomplished in a matter of months or a year of analysis, but in borderline and psychotic patients it is the major work, taking years—and its accomplishment represents an analytic achievement of the first order. In fact, as I have said it would probably be called the crucial step in establishing fundamental health and removing the danger of psychotic deterioration.

The relinquishment of this mechanism for escaping from the dilemma of infantile distress makes possible the establishment of a limited type of dependence. We have come to call this the "toilet-breast" relationship in order to designate the purely expulsive aim and part-object experience. It would appear that before the internal "toilet-breast" has been established the unavailability of an object in the outside world capable of containing such pain throws the ego back on massive projective identification with an internal object: if this fails to control the anxiety, states of schizophrenic withdrawal into delusion or autistic fragmentation, separately or in tandem, appear to be the only recourse.

But to return to the phase of the therapeutic process under discussion, I have indicated that the "heir", so to speak, to the relinquishment of massive projective identification is the "toilet-breast" dependence on an external, and eventually, on an internal object. Its establishment at times of separation begins to leave clear the central analytic period, mid-week and mid-term, for the appearance of the oedipus complex in its genital and pre-genital forms, all muddled together in what I have called the "confusion of zones and modes". This term "zones and modes" is borrowed from Erikson: his way of employing it can be found in his book *Childhood and Society* (Norton, 1951). The term "mode" is somewhat different from Freud's "aim" of instincts and more closely related to unconscious phantasy in that it would describe the interaction between an erogenous zone and its object, such as extrusion, incorporation, retention, penetration, etc. What appears with increasing force in the playroom at this time is a growing excitement of a diffuse distribution and amorphous form, seeking gratification of every conceivable sort. This is of course most clear with small children and more disturbed latency ones, but even the rigid and obsessional child will betray it in word, gesture, posture, play, graphic work and writing, if not yet in dreams. It is at this time that the analytic room changes from being either "inside" or "outside", alternately, into the place of "analysis" as distinct from all other areas and activities in the lives of both analyst and child. The "others" in the analyst's life are no longer the internal-babies of delusional jealousy but are his children, spouse, friends, enemies, balanced by figures of comparable importance if not identical significance in the child's life outside analysis.

Although it is true that the relinquishment of massive projective identification as a preferred defence enhances the distinction between the inside and outside of objects, the distinction between external reality and psychic reality is still a distant accomplishment and most of the work of this third phase of the analytic process takes place in the midst of a constant confusion and oscillation between these two worlds of object relations. For this reason dreaming and waking are much confused and the masturbatory relation with internal objects easily breaks forth with external objects as well. Only later, with the struggle to establish the feeding relation to the breast, on the threshold of the depressive position, does the economic task of differentiating internal from external press forward, that is to say when the problem of reparation takes the centre of the stage. This will be discussed in subsequent chapters. At this point it behoves us to describe and, if possible, categorise the process of movement through this chaos of zones and modes by which sufficient order will be created so as to make possible experience of introjective dependence on the feeding breast and of the ensuing genital oedipus complex with its attendant struggle for integration of bisexuality and of split-off parts.

The general structure of the transference, then, in this phase is as follows: (*a*) the central working time of the session, week and term are relatively cleared of the impingement of massive projective identification and its phenomenology, which continues to a variable degree to dominate the separations; (*b*) the projective "toilet-breast" relationship forms the dependency background of the analytic work and all excesses of psychic distress, persecutory, depressive or confusional, are expelled into the analyst by characteristic means; (*c*) the transference relation becomes flooded with excitement in which zones and modes are confused; (*d*) the introjective aspect of infantile dependence is increasingly held in a split-off position outside the analytic situation, as the oral introjective relation to the breast becomes more clearly differentiated from other zones and modes of infantile transference; (*c*) projective identification as a mechanism now functions in a less massive way, in relation to selective zones, to erase the differentiation between adulthood and childhood. Thus, it no longer serves to obviate the experience of infantile helplessness but it is used to eradicate the barriers against yearned-for gratifications in the genital and pregenital oedipal conflicts.

It would seem justifiable to speak, therefore, of this phase of analysis being dominated by desire and jealousy, rather than by the struggle against the experience of separateness, with the attendant anxieties, as in the previous phase of geographical confusion, or by the oscillation of paranoid and depressive anxieties on the threshold of the depressive position, which we shall witness in our discussion of the next phase in the therapeutic process. This means that the drive toward development is very strong in this present phase and the work with anxieties assumes a somewhat secondary position, i.e.—that we find ourselves analysing the anxieties which are manifest, trying to ascertain their origins, derived from the employment of certain mechanisms, such as splitting, projective identification, omnipotent control, denial, etc., rather than analysing the mechanisms themselves in an attempt to contact underlying anxieties. Another way of expressing this would be to say that we are analysing the omnipotence, attempting to lessen it by demonstrating the anxieties consequent upon its functioning rather than analysing the anxieties which necessitate the preservation of omnipotence of defences.*

It is, in an important way, particularly this phase of analysis which runs so "counter to all the child's ego-tendencies"† in the latency period, when a relative stability has so laboriously been built up through the employment of obsessional mechanisms in the internal situation for the sake of meeting the demands of the external situation, i.e. going to school. Therefore this phase can move very slowly, under tremendous conscious opposition in the rigid type of latency child while it goes like a whirlwind in little children and again at puberty.

Desire and jealousy also have a charm which makes this phase of analysis rather less of a strain than earlier and later phases, from the counter-transference points of view, although the constant resisting of seduction and aggression can be fatiguing and the violence of the passions rather alarming. This charm, however, begins to evaporate as the analysis progresses and order begins to reign where confusion had been before; desire gives way to arrogance and contempt for the analyst as a "toilet-mummy", a mere receptacle for pain, that is, since the attempt to keep toilet and feeding breasts separated requires that all capacity for infantile love be deployed outside the analytic situation.

It is possible to describe the most characteristic configurations of zonal and modal confusion and their juxtaposition to one another in the economics of the process. I believe that this phase can be subdivided into certain problems which have an

---

* *See* Appendix F.
† *See* Chapter on Latency in Melanie Klein's *Psycho-Analysis of Children.*

essential sequential relation to one another which I will describe as (a) problems of excitement; (b) problems of possession; and (c) problems of mutual idealisation.

Problems of excitement centre around the capacity for sensual delight and need clinically to be differentiated from the hectic excitement of the various manic states. This is in fact not difficult, for the manic state, with its core of triumph, is always of a gossamer quality, touch and go, leaving a deposit of depression behind it. The excitement of sensuality seeks body contact, the state of mutual exclusiveness, the per-petuation of bliss to eternity. My view is that its essence is genitalisation combined with orgiastic impotence. This derives from the sensitivity and sensual delight clustering about the penis-clitoris and the vagina-anus, stimulated by the tickling, touching, tapping technique, as distinguished from the rubbing-penetrating type of masturbatory activity associated with the problems of possession and manic reparation, and related to sadism and projective identification.*

The oedipal phantasy underlying this area of sensuality envisages a polymorphous part-object conjugation taking place between the parents as a virtually continuous process. Natur-ally the bed-time situation is its focus and the representation of bed situations finds infinite variation in play, drawing and behaviour in the playroom. The skin as a zone or organ in its own right, as distinct from the orifices of the body, asserts itself, demands a genitalised array in tickling, stroking, warm bathing, sun bathing, picking, scratching, etc. The eyes as both passive and active genitalised zones come forward in penetrating types of looking, and conversely passive experience of traumatising sights—and of course eye rubbing and blinking as masturbatory activities.

Very little sensual interest centres on the body products in this area of zonal problems, but anxious concern envelops them as they may be scrutinised for evidence of damage done to the body by masturbation, experienced as punishment rather than as states of persecution by damaged or bad objects in psychic reality. One might think that Jones' concept of "aphanisis", or incapacity for pleasure, has a special application here and may be a diffuse representation of a primitive form of

* *See* Appendix G.

castration anxiety—i.e.—that the masturbatory zone is punished by withdrawal of its sensual capacity, for instance in urethral irritation.

The major anxieties connected with the diffuse genitalisation are, however, those consequent on the outbreaks of sadism subsequent to frustration, whether these be expressed by attacks on external objects or by masturbatory attacks on internal ones. It seems to me that projective identification is very little active in relation to this problem because, far from feeling incapable of sensual delight in comparison with the adults, children often feel superior. As a result the anxiety consequences of projective identification such as claustrophobia, hypochondria, etc., are also little in evidence. What is so prominent—it relates to this sense of superiority—is the tendency to narcissistic organisation* under the slogan that "the children have more fun in the nursery than mummy and daddy have in their bedroom". This, I think, is the main defensive aspect of the capacity for diffuse genital excitement and until it is diminished by differentiation of the zones and their functions, a very great obstacle to advance in the transference process can exist.

The lessening of this sensuality, with its tendency to promote a narcissistic type of infantile arrogance, brings forth more fully what I am calling the *problem of possession* in this phase of zonal and modal confusions. As a primitive form of love the possessiveness fundamentally centres on the breast as an introjective object in its most essential and precious sense in its capacity to restore the objects of psychic reality for the baby. But these are not the qualities which are the focus of the possessiveness at this time. The possessiveness here is far more derivative on the one hand from the tendency to jealousy and on the other hand from the sensuality already described. For these reasons it tends to focus on the socially-visible qualities of the breast whose possession, as an object, can project jealousy and envy into others. The attribute of this excellence is the beauty of the breast which qualifies it magnificently for confusion, or equation, with buttocks, eyes, cheeks, legs, hands—every shapely, symmetrical, colourful or sensually textured part. Projective identification with these parts of his

* See Appendix H.

object enhances the child's vanity about its own body, but also, as with the sensuality, a competition between the world of children and adults may be structured in which the claim, not totally unconfirmed by adult behaviour, that children are more beautiful than grown-ups, plays a central role. The hairlessness of the body is flaunted, so much in contrast to the other area of intense envy of the pubic hair and its equation with sexual potency.

Since possession of these beautiful parts of the object is so central, the means of taking possession and of retention and defence of the possessed, form an overwhelming preoccupation, contributing, along with the equation of the part-objects with one another, to a confusion of related zones, mouth-vagina-anus-hand-eye-tongue-penis.

Because the working of projective identification equates the body products with those of the object, some degree of pre-occupation with products is evinced, but not so prominently as later on. At this point particularly the beauty is central; feces=baby, flatus=music of mother's voice, the colour of the urine=mothers golden hair, etc. In other words, a confusion of the sensuality of the various zones and their corresponding objects equates nose=mouth=eye=ears=hands and encourages the idealisation of the body products as objects of this quasi-aesthetic appreciation.

One can see the progressive curtailment of the narcissism which has taken place up to this point. The differentiation of self and object has been achieved by analysis of the geo-graphical confusions; the sensual autonomy of the nursery has been challenged by analysis of the genitalisation; and now the vanity has been undermined by the interpretation of the claims of possessing the beautiful objects of desire. The urine, feces and other body products have been divested of much of their sensual idealisation; the feebleness of the infantile self to sustain itself has been revealed, and the stage is set for an approach to its severely denied and split-off intro-jective dependence.

But before this battle can take place a skirmish of mounting fury must replace the relatively delightful bacchanalia of sensuality and beauty which has been going on in the trans-ference. The last-ditch stand of narcissistic "independence" takes the form of denial of the need of an object of introjective dependence by virtue of an assertion of mutuality.

In a certain sense this takes the form of driving a bargain, seeking a compromise between rampant narcissism and full-blown infantile dependence. The bid which is put forward is for a mutual idealisation, a closed system, a secret society. "We are symbiotic" is its slogan and many parents fall into the trap. Now the emphasis moves into the sphere of body-products and their idealisation, as the splitting-off of the feeding-breast lessens. Its tendency to union with the toilet-breast and its dependence upon the father's penis brings the central struggle of the genital oedipus complex onto the horizon. But this union is opposed; and a very dangerous tendency exists at this point in the transference for a reversal of the splitting, i.e.—to bring the feeding breast into the playroom and to split-off the toilet-breast elsewhere. Naturally this produces a plethora of aggressive acting out, more frequently seen in a protracted form in the analysis of adults than in children, whose real love for, and dependence on, their parents militates against it.

This mutual idealisation represents a reparativeness which which must be differentiated from that seen later, at the threshold of the depressive position. At this point the differentiation of internal and external reality is still very poorly drawn in the infantile object relations and the tendency exists still to eradicate the significance of the difference between adult and infantile worlds in contrast to the later urgency to become grown-up in a hurry.

The zonal and modal confusions which are utilised to seduce the object into this mutual idealisation and closed system .of mutual gratification centre, as I suggested before, on the body products; urine=semen=saliva, feces=penis=baby. The zonal confusions such as nipple=penis=tongue and mouth=vagina= anus thus enter in with an emphasis on equating the constellations: nipple-giving-milk-to-mouth = penis-giving-semen-to-vagina=tongue-giving-saliva-to-breast= anus-giving-feces-to-pot-mummy-smiling-at-baby=baby-cooing-to-mummy, etc.,

It is at this point, in the intensified separation reactions which accompany this conflict, that the concept of inside babies again comes into fierce prominence, as it had in the phase of geographical confusions, but because the emphasis is on idealisation rather than on the denial of infantile helplessness, it is jealousy rather than envy, which is to the fore. This forces upon the patient the idea of the analyst's home-children but now as loved, real, good children, rather than cosseted cherubim.

As the analyst systematically resists seduction, interprets the splitting and idealisation, reduces the zonal confusions and equations and confronts the mounting rage and anxiety, the stage is set, as I view it, for the struggle to establish the feeding breast, the often prolonged and by no means always successful battle on the threshold of the depressive position, which will be discussed in the next chapter.

To review briefly, I have put forward here not only the concept of a phase of zonal and modal confusion as the central theme in the transference but have attempted to describe its organisation in the light of the struggle to curtail the narcissism and bring the infantile structures within reach of the experience of dependence on the mother and father as a parental couple. The suggested organisation of this phase entails a sequence of problems which stand in an essential economic relation to one another, the first being a tendency to diffuse genitalisation of all zones with attendant excitement and quest for sensual gratification. The second is an idealisation of the beauty of the part-objects and a quest for their exclusive possession. The third is an attempt to form a closed system of mutual idealisation with an object through idealisation of the reparative qualities of the body products.

The work in this phase is attended, as in the previous phase, by a great deal of acting in and out of the transference, in child and adolescent as well as in adult cases. Since partners to the narcissistic organisation are required in the acting out, siblings are pressed into service by children as are friends or spouse by the adult. But intractable resistance is a rarity, hardly seen except where *folie a deux* with a parent has previously existed as the source of the psychopathology. The most protracted resistance in this phase occurs in the patients with well-formed patterns of delinquency, perversion or addiction. But even in such cases progress will be made in sorting the confusions if the analyst can persevere, until the real struggle of the next phase sets in in earnest.

4

CHAPTER IV

THE THRESHOLD OF THE DEPRESSIVE POSITION

In the first three chapters I have described my tentative reconstruction of the *natural history of the analytic process*, a sequence dictated by the economics of psychic life, as it unfolds in analysis when *adequately presided over and adequately supported* by environmental factors outside the analysis proper. It is important to bear in mind that this whole concept of the natural history of the analytic process cannot be used in the moment-to-moment work of the consulting room. It is not a tactical conception but a strategic one, which, like W. R. Bion's grid,* is for use in mobilising and preserving the therapeutic vitality of the analyst. Perhaps it is also of use in the retrospection which is required for the making of scientific communications.

It has been described how the gathering together of infantile transference tendencies makes possible a systematic clarification of confusional states, in the course of which there takes place a relinquishment of narcissism (as a principle of organisation) in favour of dependence on internal primal good objects (and externally the analyst and analytic setting and process). I have emphasised that the growth of actual dependence, and the growth of its acknowledgement, proceed independently, the projective relation to the mother (toilet breast) being more easily established than the introjective (feeding breast) which we are about to study. This in turn is more easily accepted than the necessary role of the paternal penis. This conflict, the oedipus complex, at genital and pregenital levels, forms the core of that striving for integration and *in*dependence, which we will study in the next chapter.

* *Elements of Psycho-Analysis* (Heinemann), 1964.

32

The various constellations of transference described separately in each chapter are visible in more minute form in all four time dimensions of the analytic process, an example of which will be seen in Chapter VII. Lastly a reminder that different constellations of psychopathology will cause greater or lesser difficulty of working through in different phases of the process but that it is not conceivable that any phase can be by-passed, since each phase is seen to have an absolute metapsychological dependence on the adequate working through of the previous one.

In the chapter on the "sorting of zones and modes", I have traced a tentative comprehension of the sequence of events by which erotisation, intolerance to separation, possessive jealousy and their attendant confusions about object relations permit an approach to the breast as an object of infantile introjective dependence. It is always, I think, a shock in analysis to discover that this difficult work of preparation, calling for such ingenuity, steadfastness and toleration, is not suddenly rewarded by the patient's acceptance of a trusting dependence on the analytic process. In fact, quite the opposite seems to occur, namely the appearance of *dis*trust, not of the benevolence but of the strength and adequacy of the analyst as a good breast. On the one hand it appears *de novo* from a matrix of denial that any need of an object of dependence exists. On the other hand this distrust replaces the more paranoid type of distrust which had existed under the influence of geographical and zonal confusions. From an attitude of "I don't need you" the transference proceeds, disappointingly, to a position of "You are not what I need". In a word, from denial to negation, in Freud's terms.

It is a peculiar and protracted struggle that takes place in analysis at this time. I have applied the word "struggle" here for the first time, in these chapters, for a very special reason. It is a time in which the analyst will find that his resources of fighting spirit and perseverance are more specifically called upon, as compared to earlier times when his capacity to bear the projection of psychic pain was probably the most requisite quality of character taxed by the analytic work.

Due to the earlier therapeutic achievements, confusional states and their attendant acting out tendency has been diminished, and infantile life is better differentiated from adult processes and better contained in the analysis and dream life. Consequently the patient experiences periods of well-being and harmonious external and internal relations which not only loosen his feeling of need for analysis but even carry with them a certain forgetfulness about the earlier miseries, inadequacies and confusions. Like the student who returns from his first year of university to find his father greatly improved intellectually in the interim, the patient now finds the world to have improved, rather than himself in relation to it. He is rather astounded, therefore, to note the para-doxical vehemence of his reactions to separation and his growing uneasiness about the analyst's health and vitality. The "latency period" of the analytic process has arrived and is often attended in adults, as well as with the children, by an insidious impoverishment of material and an unspoken attitude of waiting-for-termination, as if this would be some release from bondage granted by the benevolent analyst-despot. In addition a certain "analytic stupidity" tends to set in, as processes of externalisation of internal situations begin to blanket and flavour object relations in certain areas outside the analysis, bringing in its wake an atmosphere of denial of psychic reality. Pathological acting out due to projective identification and confusional states is replaced by more benign and reality-adjusted acting out due to externali-sation at a less part-object level.*

It is generally true that by this time in analysis, which is unlikely to be attained in less than two or three years with children and four or five with adults, the perversions have been relinquished, compulsive masturbatory activities have departed from waking life and the destructive attacks on internal objects occur primarily in the sleep-life. But none-theless the security of the internal world has *not* been established and termination is unthinkable. Character structure is obsessional and a pervasive delinquency and reserve, if not secrecy *per se*, is to be noted.

The material of the sessions reveals the activity of the destructive infantile part fighting a last-ditch stand to preserve the remnants of narcissism by cynical attacks on the truth

* *See* Appendix A.

and by aggravation of depressive anxieties with distrust, mockery and jealousy-provoking innuendo, to a point that the distress is often indistinguishable to the patient from a state of persecution. At infantile levels this takes the form of an organisation of the infantile parts in what I call "the agony in the nursery", to adopt Thurber's phrase, at every experience of separation. Several central themes of the cynical attacks on trust can be noted, each infantile theme being also voiced in transference form against the analyst and the analytic situation. (*a*) "Parents abandon their children to indulge sexually and analysts abandon their patients at week-ends and holidays." But this cannot be evidenced since parents and analysts do not make themselves unavailable and when needed provide a surrogate to tend and supervise. In non-hospitalised patients this surrogate is, by and large, whether with adult or child patient, the most mature aspect of the patient's personality armed with insight and bulwarked by whatever strength and understanding is available from the immediate environment, especially the parents. (*b*) "Out-of-sight is out-of-mind." Parents (and analysts) do not think about their children (and patients) when away. But this is clearly refuted by the liveliness of their recall of previous events (and sessions) and unaltered nature of their contact, while the children (and patients) clearly demonstrate a deterioration both of recall and contact. It is clear that it is the children (and patients) who treat their parents (and analysts) in an "out-of-sight out-of-mind" manner. (*c*) "Parents (and analysts) only look after their children (and patients) because they must by law or custom (ethics, reputation and economic need) or to aggrandise themselves with their peers (in order to gather material for books, papers and lectures)." But the law (and ethics) would not prevent parents (and analysts) from handing their unwanted burdens to surrogates, in the final instance to the community. Bad children (and patients) could easily be replaced by good ones by procreation or adoption (by filling vacancies). (*d*) "The parent-child (analyst-patient) division is a class-structure in which strength, possession, and other forms of power are utilised to tyrannise, exploit and control." But this cannot be so, as the children (patients) harm each other the moment they are not subject to adult control and supervision, and they have neither wealth nor services to offer their parents (analysts). The fees paid to an analyst do not come from the infantile structures but are paid by the adult part of the personality, just as in child analysis. It is a class-structure indeed, but based on real differences in capacity and, above all, in capacity for responsibility. The children are debarred from sexual activity because they are *genitally* incapable and merely use their genitals to express pregenital impulses and phantasies. (*e*) "Parental roles (analytic interpretations and techniques) are arbitrary, merely rationalised despotism, guesswork and covert threats." But this cannot be so as the punishments involve only a withdrawal of services, the rules are only suggested methods of procedure, and the interpretations are suggested formulations for comprehending the data at hand. The analyst's refusal to leave the field of his own professional functioning (technique and setting) cannot be considered coercive, though it is open to the suspicion of being aggressive. (*f*) "If parents (analysts) loved their children (patients) they would be more concerned to keep them happy." But it is clear that parents (and analysts) do not love their children (patients), in the first instance, but manifest toward them a capacity for tender concern derived from their other (internal and external) relations, a by-product, as it were. This tender concern is, truly, more centered on promoting development than on affording pleasure or shielding from pain, as it naturally looks forward to eventual release from its burdens, be they ever so enjoyable. Love, on the other hand, must be deserved. (*g*) "Even if the difference between good and evil be admitted, beauty and goodness don't always go together, nor does goodness seem to win out in the struggle." But this, while seemingly true in the external world, is not true of psychic reality, from whence all feeling of security, vitality and capacity for joy must derive.*

Such are some of the lines of attack on trust in the good objects which can be seen to overwhelm the good parts of the infantile organisation during separation, and to lead to temporary regression and masturbatory attacks on internal objects. No period of analysis teaches us the elements of

* *See* Appendix I.

technique so well as the work at the threshold of the depressive position. Because every facet of attitude, upon which the technique must be based, is under hostile scrutiny by a destructive infantile part of the patient's personality, the analyst is continually put to the test of clarifying, for himself and his patient, the rationale of the setting, demeanour and mechanics of communication.

Probably the most important differentiation in this respect is that between responsibility and omnipotence on the analyst's part. Again it is with children that the greatest clarity can be achieved, since the primary divisions of responsibility, parental, legal, medical, psycho-analytical—are in themselves well separated. But, while it is clear that an analyst *can* only carry psycho-analytical responsibility, the boundaries of this are far from defined where the analytic process carries with it a danger to the patient's physical health, physical safety and integration in the community.

While the destructive parts are kept split off, which means they will be represented in dream, play and association by figures other than the self, very little progress can be made to ameliorate the constant leaking away of trust. It is rather the fact of the splitting and projecting which must be investigated. And here a most fascinating difficulty can be seen to arise, namely that the "good" child-parts keep the "bad" ones split off, i.e. out of the family, away from the breast, primarily out of jealous possessiveness.* The possessiveness is rationalised as a sense of injustice, concern for the safety of the good objects or high ideals of purity. In fact it can for this reason often be a long struggle to bring the destructive voices into the consulting room so as to challenge the analyst directly. When it begins to happen in the sphere of separation experiences, before and after breaks, it leaves the intervening analytic time free for working over oedipal material, at both genital and pregenital levels, to a degree which had not been possible before.

Even more important, the opportunity for demonstrating the relation of internal and external reality arises. By this time in analysis a sufficient horizontal splitting† has been brought about so that the adult part of the personality is

---

* *See* my paper on "Somatic Delusion", *I.S.P.A.*, Vol. XLV, p. 294, 1964.
† *See* Appendix J.

clearly distinguished from those pseudo-adult states of mind consequent on massive projective identification which may still at times occur. The adult structure is very sensitive, through its introjective identification, to the state of the internal objects. The disturbances of well-being, both physical and mental, of the internal objects, due either to omnipotent control and separation from one another (obsessional) or attacks (masturbatory, mainly still by projective identification) are promptly reflected in the physical and mental state of the adult self. It therefore becomes a regular experience that the analysis brings relief, due to the introjective relation to the external breast in the infantile transference.

This process, whose details can best be followed in dreams both in adults and children, builds, session by session, the acknowledgement of the primacy of psychic reality. This development at mid-week, stands in striking contrast to those sessions surrounding breaks which are dominated by the destructive infantile structures, with their cynicism, dishonesty, promulgation of self-pity and ruthless attacks on the analyst's capacity to think. At no time is the concreteness of splitting processes more starkly evident.

As I have indicated elsewhere,* this period of the analysis sees the emergence into the forefront of the material of problems related to splitting in the self and its resolution, as well as some degree of lessening of the severity of the splitting. But the fear of the destructive bullying parts and the phenomenon of cowardice do pose a grave problem in the separations. Panics about somatic symptoms may arise, as somatic delusional trends and hypochondriacal phenomena are likely to mingle together, both at a relatively obsessional level. To complicate further the persecutory aspect of depressive anxieties met with at this "threshold of the depressive position", in patients with addictive trends or with perversions, there may arise the problem of terror, as a form of overwhelming and paralysing fear, connected with dead objects, particularly with the mother's babies in psychic reality.† There seems to be no

---

* *See* my paper "The Differentiation of Somatic Delusions from Hypochondrical," *Int. J. Psa.*, Vol. XLV.

† To be expanded in a forthcoming paper, to be read to the Int. Congress o Psycho-Analysis, 1967, Copenhagen. *See* Appendix C.

possibility of further progress into the depressive position until this conflict is resolved. It turns out to be a complication of the problem of infantile possessive jealousy and greed toward the breast, which at this time in the analysis becomes more and more the central force opposing integration. It must be understood that integration is a problem on two levels. At the infantile level it is a problem of sharing the good objects with other parts of the self, experienced as siblings (problems of possessive jealousy) as well as with each other (oedipus complex). This latter happening is of course accompanied by a lessening of splitting and idealisation of both self and objects in psychic reality as the depressive position becomes more firmly established. At the adult level, on the other hand, the problem is one of responsibility for psychic reality, the acceptance of which, in the form of the commencement of self-analytic effort, lays the groundwork for eventual termination of analysis, as we shall see in the next chapter.

I have been discussing the central problem of the "threshold of the depressive position", namely the concerted attack on the strength of the good object that is mounted by the most split-off destructive parts of the infantile personality. In this process the severity of the splitting is gradually diminished and attacks upon the breast relation in the transference which originally took the form of distressing body sensations in the consulting room gradually metamorphose into more mental and eventually verbalisable form.* For instance, a little boy whose approach to the breast took the form of rhythmical ball-bouncing in which the analyst had to keep score, experienced, over a period of months, a sequence of attacks on his concentration, and therefore his success. At first these took the form of tickling sensations in his body, later of dirty jokes which would come into his mind and force him to giggle and finally of verbalised suspicions of a sexual connection between his mother and the analyst which would cause sudden outbreaks of destructive attacks on the ball, the room and the analyst. In his biting of the ball, scratching of the analyst's head, in lightning attacks and kicking at his genitals, the hatred of the penis-in-the-breast configuration could be seen clearly.

* *See* my paper on "Somatic Delusion".

This configuration* forms the focal point of the attack on the strength of the breast and opens the whole area of the genital oedipus complex to a detailed exploration. As I have mentioned earlier, the core of the perversions and addictions, even though their acting out had been earlier lessened or even abandoned, only comes under scrutiny at this time when the primitive forms of voyeurism into the breast,† and of omnipotent projective attacks by way of the eyes, the wind and the flatus, declare themselves openly. The opposition to the role of the internal mother's many inside-penises that produce her strength to resist these attacks on her structure, on her functions and her internal babies, may form a prolonged and difficult struggle: it is probably the most frequent cause of the impasses in therapeutic progress which dog the history of this phase of analysis. The terrifying anxieties which result from these most primitive oral and anal sadistic attacks on the breast readily lend themselves to attenuation through addiction to the omniscience of the destructive parts of the self, in lieu of resolution by reparation through the services of the good objects, which is always attended with severe depressive pains.

The roles of the father's penis and testicles begin to be clearly distinguished from the many roles of the mother's internal penises‡ and the basis to be laid for the proper differentiation of male and female, some of which had already been worked out during the sorting of the zonal confusions. But now the full acknowledgement of the creative and reparative role of the father is possible. The oedipus complex in its full genital crescendo comes to the fore of the transference and with it the final step into the depressive position with its shift in values from ego-centric to object-centered solicitude.

Thus far I have discussed mainly the central problem of this phase of analysis, namely the establishment of trust in the capability of the good objects, especially the mother's breast, to perform their functions of reparation and protection, while still withstanding attacks from bad objects and destructive parts of the self. It is in the repeated rhythmic experience

---

* *See* my paper "A Contribution to the Metapsychology of Cyclothymic States", *Int. S. of Psycho-Analysis*, Vol. XLIV, p. 83, 1963.

† *See* Appendices C and F.

‡ *See* Appendix E.

of destruction and restoration, of despair and hope, of mental pain and joy, that the experience of gratitude arises, from which the bond of love for, and concern about, the good objects are forged. As the depressive position is penetrated more deeply, the threshold problem of being able to accept forgiveness *by* good objects for attacks and defections becomes replaced by the problem of being able to *forgive oneself* for past breaches of good faith. This, along with the genital oedipus complex, forms the central theme of the phase of weaning or termination.

This rhythmical experience of reparation and destruction, of distress and relief through contact with the analytic breast, is reflected in the play of children by the new role of rhythm in their analytic participation: the bouncing of balls; the performing of acrobatic activities which declare and defy their fear of heights; the oscillation between patterned and figured drawings; the representation in play of situations challenging trust such as learning to swim or learning arithmetic tables; oscillation in closeness and distance to the body of the analyst or to the couch of the playroom, alternation of dreamy with alert states of mind; all these and innumerable other manifestations capture, or rather recapture, the experience of the breast-feed relation. Most noticeable of all is the development of interest in the analyst's words, and of course a consequent urge toward verbalisation as the main avenue of communication. While earlier the analyst's interpretive activity may have been greeted with indifference, jamming, echoing or fingers-in-ears, a hush now comes when he speaks, actions suspended and eyes to his eyes, sometimes with the slightly dazed inner look which may last a few moments after the interpretation is ended.

Even the very young children, now 5 or 6 years of age, can bring dreams by this time, as the experiences of waking and sleeping are better differentiated. Play with toys, equipment of the room and involvement with the body of the analyst give way to graphic representation, associations, story writing and discussion. But it is a time of extremely sensitive balance, with children as with adults, for the analytic work at the mid-week times of close contact with the analytic breast is under the constant hostile scrutiny of the destructive infantile parts.

This cynical vigilance is directed toward the analyst's technique in particular, so that any gratuitous breach may be followed by severe regression, while the approaches to breaks are accompanied by systematic attempts, through seduction, trickery, aggression and threat, to break the setting of the analysis. Manic reparation which earlier was directed outward toward the toys, equipment and analyst are now more directed inward. A current of pseudo-analysis, following the verbal forms of interpretation but grotesque in their caricaturing of content, may be heard even from the smaller children but especially in the adolescent patients. Projective identification with the nipple will usually be found to underlie this activity and may, even in children as so frequently in adults, be acted out in pseudo-analytic practice with siblings and friends. As such it stands in contrast to the general current of secrecy which is dictated by the possessiveness toward the breast.

This possessiveness we will study further in the next chapter on The Weaning Process, but one aspect of it is particularly germane to the "threshold", namely the requirement of the analyst, and of analysis generally, that it be beyond mockery and contempt. This is part of the later phenomenology of the "agony in the nursery", when trust in the goodness and strength of the breast has been well established but the oedipus complex is far from resolution. In almost daily analytic experience of relief of despair and return of hopefulness the power of the external breast to repair the internal situation has produced love, but not yet the strength to defend this love. The beauty of the object is very central here, and when its exclusive possession is not being flaunted in order to project the pains of oedipal jealousy into sibling parts of the self represented in the outside world, its possession is being carefully hidden from the greedy or mocking siblings. A little girl whose little brother usually was with her mother waiting in the car at the end of sessions, used frantically in the last moments of the hour to scribble a picture to take to him. It had several functions: to placate his curiosity; to create a mock sharing of the analysis; but above all to provide her older brother, who would see it when they reached home, with a false target for his mocking attacks, borne now by the little deceived brother rather than by herself.

Before leaving this phase of the analytic process I wish to stress that it is the area of most frequent intractable resistance in the analytic work, with adults as well as children. The reason for this is, to my mind, a purely economic one, despite its structural aspects or manifestation. The threshold of the depressive position is a turning point in the economics of mental pain in the analytic process, when the waning of persecutory anxieties gives way to the waxing of depressive distress. At ebb an experience of general well-being tends to belie the extreme dependence on the external analytic breast, covered by a deeply unconscious denial of its inevitable and eventual relinquishment. Each step deeper into the depressive position, with its shift from self-interest to concern for the objects, brings more urgently the realisation of both the dependence and the eventual weaning. The "struggle", as I have called it, in this phase of the analysis, is against the furious drive for compromise to maintain the *status quo* at the ebb tide of pain. This takes the form of the "turncoat phenomenon", mummy's baby in the daytime and one of the gang at night, as it were—*ad infinitum*. It can be easily seen that the denial of time as a relentless unidirectional phenomenon in the outside world plays a central role in this, as time is dealt with concretely as either circular or oscillating. In contrast, as we shall see in the next chapter, the experience of being given the "time of the analyst's life" plays a great role in the acceptance of weaning.

CHAPTER V

THE WEANING PROCESS

As mentioned in the previous chapter, when the feeding relation to the breast at infantile levels begins to be acknowledged in the experience of the transference, termination immediately looms on the horizon and the fear of premature ending plays a role in all the subsequent work. This fear interacts at infantile levels with the depressive concern for "mother's babies" and dominates the struggle toward integration as a life-long task. Its counterpart at the most adult level arises as an aesthetic and intellectual appreciation of the analytic process even in young children, driving the patient to "give the next fellow his turn" and to spare the analyst unnecessary work—the "time of his life".

This latter point, being the main focus of the therapeutic alliance in approaching cooperatively the decision for termination, may occupy us first so that we can return to the infantile problems in a more organised way. By the time that this phase has been reached in analysis, even with young children, the cooperation and interest in the analytic work is astonishing, not only embracing control of acting out and a continual collection of material for analysis from the events of daily life, but an enthusiasm for dream analysis which comes from the full acknowledgement of psychic reality and its primacy for their states of mind. The repeated experience of awakening from sleep in a mood which cannot be shaken off until the analytic session resolves it, brings forth both conviction and gratitude which sets in motion the urge to self-analysis out of useful sparing motives, in contrast to the envious or competitive motivation which was the driving force in such pseudo-self-analytic attempts during phases two and four in particular.

Thus an adult appreciation of the beauty and goodness of the analytic process and method of discovering the truth can begin to sort itself out from the infantile transference which seems to attach itself so tenaciously to the person of the analyst. He can now be seen to preside over the process in a way which reasonably yields to the assumption of these responsibilities by the patient himself. Something akin to the workings of analytic supervision is fairly approached which can be facilitated by reserve on the analyst's part. The experience will accrue, most typically, on the Monday session: the persecuted state of mind that would have 6 months earlier required the analyst's hard work through Tuesday now will be resolved in the first 15 minutes of the Monday session by the patient himself—if the analyst will wait for him to do so.

I am particularly impressed by the experience of the beauty of the process which regularly emerges, first in a detached form but easily drawn back to its origin. For instance in an early morning session of a fourteen year old girl, recovering, after seven years analysis, from a deeply schizoid quality of character, a long interpretation had been made linking the immediate material with some of two weeks previous and also with drawings from three years earlier in the analysis. She was silent for a rather long time, then said, with unusual emotion for her, that the sky had become a most beautiful bright blue. She readily agreed that this was unlikely to be an accurate perception of a concrete external object as she was looking through a lace curtain and it had been heavily overcast when she had come to the session thirty minutes earlier. A link at infantile levels to her mother's blue eyes could also be traced, as we had been occupied with the analysis of some of her own difficulties in perceiving very near and very distant objects, felt to contrast with her mother's clear-sightedness in human relations.

Similarly the new interest in dreaming and dream analysis which appears at this time reflects the patient's altered relationship to the nocturnal mental life. A spectrum of dream structure can be assembled in something of the following way: (a) dreams in which the patient is watching a film, looking at a painting, etc., in a detached position in relation to a process whose reality is denied; (b) the person is watching events but in no way involved; (*c*) he is observing events as an interested bystander but not committed in relation to contending factions; (*d*) he is a child engaged with other children and adults; (*e*) he is a child engaged with other children who either are siblings or are felt as parts of himself; (*f*) he is an adult engaged with adults and children who are recognised as parts of himself. This spectrum reflects psychic structure and types (*e*) and (*f*) can only be expected regularly when responsibility for integration has developed in the depressive position within the sphere of internal good objects, especially the breast at the infantile level. There may even develop the type of dream monitoring in which analytic thought accompanies the sleeping experience of the dream and may be seen to influence the outcome, actually utilising insights gained from previous dream analysis. I have observed this as early as puberty and would not be surprised to find it even at an earlier age.

These phenomena reflect the two basic attainments of this phase of analysis, namely the establishment internally of the infantile introjective dependence on the mother's breast, and secondly, the differentiation of levels by which the most mature segment of the personality, through its introjective identification, begins to develop its capacities for introspection and analytic thought and responsibility.

These accomplishments set the stage for the work of termination on the one hand and the interminable work of striving toward integration through analysis and self-analysis on the other. I wish to discuss this now in some detail, before turning to the final topic of our inquiry, the unhappy problem so frequently encountered, *interruption* of analysis. I will choose first the work of termination, or the "weaning process", for it is in its matrix prior to termination and in its honour, "in memoriam", one might say, thereafter, that the work of integration proceeds. Perhaps a candid word would be in order regarding the background of what follows, which to some extent applies to all of the present chapter, in contrast to the earlier ones. The conclusions it puts forward are compounded of trends seen in my own cases and those I have supervised which have been brought to a relatively satisfactory termination. The concept can hardly apply to children, who still have before them the major biological and social upheaval of puberty to face. But the same is also true to some degree of adult patients whose parents are still alive, so that they have not yet been confronted with the primal mourning situation. Without having traversed these great upheavals it is virtually an impossibility for full resolution of the transference to take place by way of internalisation, since some measure of dependence upon the external parents is bound to remain active.

As I have said, weaning presents itself as a real possibility with the first *acknowledged* experience of introjection at the breast in the transference and thence hangs over the heads of patient and analyst alike. It is of interest that this moment is often very clearly discernible in the material either as a conscious anxiety of being hurried or as an intellectual concept of the analyst having a "waiting list". But it may be months or even years before the weaning process itself begins to take shape: this also is clearly distinguishable. It shows itself as a striking change one holiday, usually the long summer break, from which the patient returns obviously having made a step forward in the interim, in contrast to the usual regression. From then on almost every week-end and holiday break is apprehended by the patient in a depressive vein, as a task and a trust, rather than as an abandonment.

The depressive situation, at bottom the death-of-the-breast,* runs thread-like through all the material now. Attention to the analyst's physical and mental state, the urge to differentiate the person of the analyst in the outside world from the transference figures projected by psychic reality, and sensitivity to intrusion upon the analytic process from without, all become intensified, or may appear for the first time. An early-morning adult patient for weeks insisted that I really did look "fresher" and "happier" after his session than before, though he was reluctant to take full credit for this change himself. A child patient now exhibited despair and apathy whenever her mother brought her late and felt that great pressure existed in the family for her to finish analysis "to give her little brother a turn", on grounds of financial limitation. She countered by insisting on coming by herself, by refusing to allow new clothes

* *See* Appendix K.

to be bought for her and by laying great stress on the fact that she had won a scholarship to the senior school.

Among children two types of behaviour seem to appear outside the analysis which are probably intended to ensure the process against premature termination by the parents. One of these is a manifest unhappiness at home contrasting with school reports of cheerfulness, cooperation, etc. The other is a quietness about the analysis that approximates to stealth, like the keeping of a private diary.

Upon this "carrying-frequency", of the weaning process, the more stormy conflicts of integration appear as a "modulation". In a certain sense it is all related to the oedipus complex, but in a manner rather different from the pregenital aspects seen variously in the third and fourth phases when zonal confusions and the approach to introjective dependence were in the forefront. At that time the reparative aspects of the parental coitus were most prominent, as they related to the restoration of damage caused by sadistic attacks which had been made out of envy and later of jealousy, particularly in connection with masturbatory habits. As more whole-object relations to internal and external figures take shape, the particular pre-occupation with the reproductive aspect of coitus now moves into prominence. This needs to be distinguished from the earlier preoccupation with the inside-babies of the internal mother which dominated, in the forms of delusional jealousy, the pregenital aspects of the oedipus complex. The split between "business and pleasure", as it were, is still maintained and only very grudgingly yielded to, in the context of a type of bargaining attitude. The parents are allowed to accomplish successfully the "business" while long begrudged the pleasure of their intercourse.

This problem of the reproductive aspect of the parental coitus has a most important relation to both the problem of integration on the one hand and to that of termination on the other. This latter is fairly obvious in its reference to the "expectation of the next baby" to take its place at mother's breast. What is less obvious is that the same experience dominates the move toward integration of severely split-off parts of the self as already indicated in the discussion of possessive jealousy in Chapter IV. This is manifest by material which reflects the process, in which the split-off part gradually alters its representation in increments something as follows: a machine becomes an animal, then a friend of the family, transforming into a sibling and finally is apprehended as a part of the self. Between the steps *friend-of-the-family* and *sibling* the storm of jealous possessiveness breaks out which resists this crucial step toward integration.* This step is often reflected in dreams and associations by new-baby-in-the-family material.

As yet we know relatively little, beyond what Melanie Klein has given us in *Envy and Gratitude*, about this process in relation to the most split-off parts of all, namely enviously destructive parts and, even more obscure, schizophrenic parts. One can, however, hardly imagine such advanced steps in integration being accomplished outside the setting of formal analysis to begin with, and without the greatest danger, of somatic disease in the first instance and schizophrenic episodes in the second. But one thing I would feel quite certain about, that, where such parts exist (and they may be universal), no possibility of their successful or reasonably safe integration could take place until the basic mental health and strength of character has been established. Any modification of technique which tends to encourage their premature appearance in the forefront of the analytic process is dangerous in the highest degree.

In reference to theory, therefore, it is clear that I am suggesting that, as we are able to practice it today, psycho-analysis cannot be expected to carry patients beyond a certain degree of reliance on correct splitting-and-idealisation of self and objects as the rock upon which mental health is founded. For instance, there seems to be evidence that every person contains a schizophrenic part which, if mental health is to be maintained, must be kept split-off and projected, since it is in its very nature impossible of integration with other parts of the personality.

Throughout these chapters I have stressed the transference process itself as the arbiter of analytic progress, trying to make clear that external criteria of the "patient-married-and-lived-happily-ever-after" type cannot find any place as a

* *See* my paper on "Somatic Delusion".

scientific description of therapeutic achievement if analysts are
to be able to compare their findings. It may seem to require
a degree of faith in our comprehension of the internal workings
of psycho-analysis which invites the accusation of fanaticism
and delusion, but I can see no way around it in the immediate
future. W. R. Bion* has proposed a grid based on a non-
analytic notation which may prove to be the answer to our
need for a cross-reference system, but until we learn to use it,
or until some elaboration of it is uniformly adopted (as
Mendeleyeff's periodic table brought such a rational notation
to chemistry), we have no alternative but to struggle toward
more accurate description of the transference situation and its
patterned progressions.

As the final step now in the description of the "natural
history" of the analytic process I would like to describe my
experience of three types of ending to analytic work, the
termination, the interruption for external reasons and the
interruption due to therapeutic impasse. I have already
described the fundamentals of the weaning process in termination. What seems to happen as the date is set for ending is a
nearly frantic process of review of the analytic process, probably akin in its alarming aspects to the regression in very
young children when their mothers are pregnant. As far as I
can make out the purpose of it seems to be not so much
consolidation of the experience in the patient's mind as a
testing by means of his own memory of the analyst's introjection of the patient as a person. For this reason a continual
"do you remember" type of inquiry is often carried on, and
in younger children, still in the playroom, the earlier configurations of play may be recapitulated, just as earlier
patterns of dreaming will appear with the adult. What will
the analyst do with the toys? Will he take as a new patient
another child or an adult? The wish to choose the next patient
from among needy friends, in particular, an unanalysed
sibling or parent; the question as to whether the patient's
material will be used for writing books or papers; the wish
for the analyst to have learned something new so that the
analytic work will have made a contribution to analytic
knowledge; and finally the apologetic admission that the

* *Elements of Psycho-Analysis* (Heinemann), 1964.

patient's ambitions lead toward almost any direction but not that of a career as an analyst; all these come forward for scrutiny in sad parade. Last and saddest of all comes the admission of wishing to restrict all future relations with the analyst—to keep him in reserve, as it were—in painful contrast to earlier phantasies of future social intimacy.

In contradistinction to this rather lovely, if painful, process, the tragic or near tragic endings by interruption must be described. Although they find their place in both child and adult work, naturally it is the interruption for external reasons that is in fact the usual outcome of child analysis, except where parents have been analysed themselves. The impasse is the most frequent outcome in our work with adults, especially with the preponderant group of borderline cases which seem to fill analytic practices and the roster of training cases.

Where parents are not in analysis themselves it is not possible to do more than guess at the motives which lie behind the great frequency of forced premature interruption against analytic advice. I am not speaking of cases which have not seen satisfactory improvement from the parental point of view but of those which have and where the need for further financial sacrifice is not easily apparent to them. Because parents are likely to take a normative and therefore symptomatic view in first bringing children to analysis, we need not assume that this is the reason for forcing interruption. In fact the circumstances often suggest that unconscious motives of jealousy, envy and states of mind based on projective identification are the true causes. Similar motives are often suggested by parental behaviour toward their child's analyst, in the form, for instance, of delayed payment, haggling over fees, attempting to reduce the number of sessions, therapeutic interventions of their own with the child, attributing improvement to influence other than analysis, especially "normal maturation". A factor of unanalysed compliance, provocation and connivance by the child often plays a part and therefore brings in an element akin to that described below as "impasse" in the analytic work.

The analytic process that accompanies the setting of a date for forced interruption is a heart-breaking one, since a systematic demolishing of all previous work begins to steam-roll all efforts of the analyst at salvage. A triumphant unintegrated destructive part of the infantile personality seems to seize control, with mockery, negativism, withholding, untruthfulness, shouting-down, icy indifference and contempt for the analyst and his work. Clearly it can only be dealt with by interpretation of the underlying despair, searching out the unconscious compliance and, above all, a stoical acceptance of the pain being projected. The one note of optimism I can offer from an overabundant experience of this sort during my years of analytic work with patients in the military service (personnel and dependents) is that a surprising amount of follow-up correspondence indicated retention of the gains and recovery of the positive aspects of the relationship.

The case of "impasse" interruption is different, for whatever defects we find in our patient's cooperation, we must accept the burden that these are *all* analytic failures, due to limitations of the science itself and our individual practice of it. I am convinced that it occurs most frequently at the threshold of the depressive position (phase IV) and that two types of factors can be identified as most culpable, but which link together very intimately. These are factors of inadequacy of setting and technique on the one hand in the analytic work and traumatic factors in the patient's developmental history, on the other. I will say no more about this subject here, as it is a huge technical area.

In closing this section I wish to repeat, as I have already done perhaps too frequently, that the attempt has been made here to describe the experience, drawn from my own work and an abundant experience of supervision of adult and child cases, of the *natural history of the analytic process over which the analyst presides*. It cannot be used in the moment to moment work of the consulting room, but only as an aid to orientation for dealing with counter-transference and for communication with colleagues.

CHAPTER VI

THE PROCESS WITH ADULT PATIENTS

It was thought better to leave the discussion of the similarities and differences between adult and child analysis until our observations on the analytical process with children had been laid before the reader, trusting that preconceptions in his mind would not prevent his persevering even if he lacks experience of child analysis. Perhaps no better way of introducing a discussion of this present topic could be found than case material dealing with the transition of method with pubertal children. Anyone who has started an analysis with a pubertal or adolescent child knows how long it takes before a psychotherapeutic process gives way to a truly analytical one. The analyst is confronted with all the limitations of child analysis regarding motivation and responsibility, without the advantages of play technique with its naivety of communication.

It is a quite different situation with a child who has been in analysis for some years of the latency period and in this context meets the mental and physical changes of puberty. At such a time we can see suspended before our eyes the two techniques, in oscillation and in competition with one another.

CASE MATERIAL

The events described cover the six months up to the onset of menstruation. This period coincided with the transition from playroom to couch at the time surrounding the child's 11th birthday, toward the end of the 4th year of an analysis which had been instituted for complaints of learning inhibition, accident proneness, screaming fits and pathologically intense jealousy of siblings.

Throughout the treatment it was characteristic of this child to have periods of work and progress followed by periods of mock-cooperation with empty repetition of the forms of previous material and abundance of physical activity in the playroom, which was often dangerous and provocative of concern. The dramatisation of unconscious phantasies was always preferred to graphic representation, but in the third year, talk and presentation of dreams became more prevalent, while activity functioned almost purely as a resistance. It was early in the fourth year that the child started to use the couch in the playroom and an eventual shift to the adult consulting room was suggested. A series of transference problems then emerged that centred on this shift as the manifest content.

The first of these problems had to do with a placating relation at infantile levels of the baby-girl part with a witch-cat part which had formerly prevented her from thinking and learning, and toward whom the showing-off baby aspect of her dare-devil motility was directed and with whom an anti-parent alliance* simmered in secrecy. Early attempts to lie on the couch in the playroom were unsuccessful due to the urge to motility of either a wall-picking (destructive) or pipe-swinging (exhibitionist) type. This diminished and was replaced by outpourings of cynical attacks on analysis, on adult values and on the concept of truth—attacks which employed a verbal facility of which we had had no knowledge earlier in the treatment (*see* Chapter IV).

But no sooner had this change occurred than the splitting of the father-transference into hero and lunatic daddies, came to the fore, made manifest in the playroom by an inability to relinquish looking at the analyst while lying on the couch. The fear of workmen in the street, men in the tube carriages, current anxiety in the transference and past distrust of her father filled dreams and associations. We could recognise evidence of a fear of being looked at, along with an emerging pubertal wish to dress up, to be looked at and "wolf-whistled".

When a blocked drain flooded the playroom and made it rather smelly, she now elected to move to the adult consulting room—temporarily, she stressed, obviously suspecting me of some Cortez-like coercion. Dreams and behaviour made it clear now that the two aspects of the split father-transference

* *See* Appendix H.

were very active and contributed to her continuation of sitting up and of looking at the analyst. In a dream she was enjoying being chased through long corridors and ever-descending stairs by a friendly ape-like creature, tricking it by jumping downstairs and hiding behind doors, until she realised that another girl was doing the same. This clearly showed that both flirtation with the hero-daddy—she had often said the analyst looked like a nice ape—and flight from the lunatic-daddy combined in determining both her behaviour and her mode of communication in which sudden changes of theme and episodes of non-attention to interpretation figured alternately, leading me a merry chase.

As Christmas approached her more manic type of un-cooperativeness gave way gradually to a depressed concern about her inability to lie down or, in fact, to "do-her-best" in the analysis. She was worried now that she was wasting time and money, that it might be better if she stopped and let her younger sibling have a turn, etc. Clearly we were moving toward her intolerance of dependence on the breast that was documented by floods of minor criticisms of her mother in external reality and a tendency to question the analyst about the rationale of his technique in its most minute facets. The suspicion in the mother transference of impro-visation, rationalisation and disorganisation differed from the earlier suspicion of hypocrisy in the father transference. A rather sophisticated claim of the you-don't-understand-us type was erected around Beatle-mania, but with little conviction. Two dreams at this time showed that lying on the couch meant accepting dependent care for her dirtied mind, in opposition to the residues of anal-masturbatory alliance with the cat-witch. In the first dream she was in the bath, wearing swimming-trunks (as her little brother always does) and lacking any breast development. Hugh (a cousin) was there. Then he was either gone or she couldn't see him and she had no swimming-trunks on and her breasts were developing. This dream suggested that some little-boy castration anxiety about the lunatic-daddy was interfering with her baby-dependence on mother, represented as Hugh ("you"—the analyst) who can be seen (when sitting up) and not seen (when lying down) respectively.

Two days later she dreamed that they (the family) were in Germany in wartime and had to go down steps to the shelter. Instead of turning left at the bottom, she continued down further steps where a stone lid had been removed from the floor. When mother called her to come up she refused and then the dream became increasingly manic—she was driving an ambulance, being fired upon, etc. Now, in reality the approach to the consulting suite is down outside steps, with the door on the left, outside of which is the cover for the drains which the patient had seen removed when workmen were cleaning them at the time that the playroom was flooded. Clearly in the dream she had allowed her mind to get into the sewer (to be preoccupied with Nazi-penises in her anal masturbatory preoccupations) rather than to have her analysis bath. This delicate balance between lying down and sitting up continued. Two weeks later she dreamed of climbing out of a muddy lake on to a grassy bank, while some sinking witches' hats suggested that others had floundered. She had had, she now revealed, her first menstrual period before the "bath" dream.

But between these events which suggested some lessening of both erotic and masochistic excitement related to the couch in the father-transference, we had a very valuable session showing some of the splitting in the mother transference which opposed her committing herself to doing-her-best in the analytic work.

On a Wednesday, two days after the "sewer" dream and two weeks before the "muddy lake" dream, she entered the consulting room, two minutes late, and was immediately hilarious about the ending of yesterday's session in which she had told the family joke about Mr. X and his admiration for peacocks. She ignored my reminder of yesterday's interpretation of the mocking-the-grownups aspect and how it was really based, for its hilarity, on the excitement about dirty words like "pee" and "cock". Instead she raced on about the shapes of thumbs in her family, whose are straight and whose are overextended. I again interpreted the preoccupation with penises which was dominating her relation to me at the moment and preventing any analytic work, as in the "chase with the ape" dream.

For a moment the hilarity broke down and a sullen, "Well, it *is* funny" replaced the banter, but quickly the manic mood returned, this time on the subject of her sister's mockery of two women of the neighbourhood who had invited her to tea and ice-cream respectively. Mimicking her sister's mimicry, she persevered in trying to make me laugh, until it became clear that the patient felt that her sister's greed and contempt had been so intense that she had neglected to get the names of her benefactresses and was thus unable to keep either appointment (with the breasts).

Oh, she'd had a dream, she suddenly recalled. No, two dreams; both about chests of drawers. In the *first*, the chest in her bedroom had its two top drawers filled with her comb and brushes and the middle large drawer was open, empty. Then she noticed that a little dark-haired girl, hidden behind the chest, was reaching round with one arm to the front of the chest, polishing the inside of this empty drawer with brown shoe-polish. (The girl, she associated, was like her image of one in a book about adopted children, a girl who had shown such aptitude for ballet.) When I interpreted that the drawer in the dream was connected with her own drawer in the chest in the playroom, she agreed it was in the same position. When I linked the analysis in the consulting room with the two top drawers, via yesterday's equation of having her hair combed with having her thoughts in order, she also agreed. But when I suggested that a mixture of concern (that the drawer in the consulting room would be messed by a new child as she used to mess it) and jealousy (that she feared a new child would treat it well, equivalent to the polishing of shoes which she herself never did), she protested that in the dream she only felt she might need the drawer some time, and anyhow she was not sure that she would not need to return to the playroom in the analysis.

In the *second* dream the white chest in the dining room at home had lots of food piled on top in readiness for a picnic— in the Chilterns—and she looked to see if there were crisps as well, which there were. I interpreted first that the dream showed that her relation to the breast-mother in the analysis was being split, that the analyst was only allowed to be the bathing, toileting and cleaning mother, not the delicious picnic-hills mother who was kept attached to her mother at home. The result was that in the dream and probably in reality as well she was behaving in a particular infantile way, always looking for the faults (are there crisps?) before acknowledging the virtues (all the other delicacies exhibited) of the breast. This related to the constant critical way that the witch-cat baby part of her always scrutinised and criticised my technique. I suggested that sitting on the couch rather than lying down tended to preserve this split between toilet-mummy here and feeding-mummy at home (*see* Chapter III).

She left protesting that she seldom complained about the food at home any more and hardly ate sweets between meals at all. But she did love crisps.

In this material the transference situation has been caught, as it were, at a hovering time, on the threshold of the depressive position as described in Chapter IV. The first four years of analysis had traversed serious confusional states due to projective identification and zonal confusions, the latter especially centering on a defective splitting between good and bad in herself wherein particularly a severe anus-vagina and feces-penis confusion had predominated. Work, particularly in the third year, had brought an increased differentiation from this cat-witch part of herself revealed as holding in thrall at infantile levels her intellect and capacity for love. The work of detaching this part from its projected position inside her sister and "bad" friends had been a tedious one indeed but had contributed very much to the lessening of her hyperactivity in the playroom and to the resultant increase of verbalisation and available intelligence for cooperation in the analytic work. This transition is nicely illustrated in a session which had occurred some nine months before the previous material, at the time of an approaching holiday break which aroused her preoccupation with my supposed children. It was a time when she was flushed with excitement and conflict on two accounts; one was her recent participation in a theatrical performance and the other was her ballet lessons, both of which had caused some disruption of usual analytic times.

Suddenly, in the middle of a Wednesday session, while lying on the couch in the playroom, she remembered a dream and was pleased, for it had been some weeks since she last remembered one. At first it bubbled forth, "I was at the table and the cook put down a little jelly and then I was stroking the cat, only it was in a different place". When the analyst began to question, she became impatient and leaping from the couch seized a piece of paper to draw the arrangement, showing that it was at school lunch. At first she had been at the side of the table, but later she was at the head in the prefect's place. "The cook, you know, one of the women who serve the food—I don't know if she cooks it—I didn't even see her in the dream—she put down a little paper cup full of jelly—see! Here! (marking it on the paper), for us to see if we liked it and wanted a lot or a little when the sweet came. I wanted a lot—of course! Then, I don't know how, I was sitting in the prefect's place and the cat (here she leaped onto the table, portraying a purring, back-arching puss, stroking herself sensuously) was on the table and I was petting it. *I don't know what it means!*" (leaping on to the analyst, en route to the floor).

The analyst interpreted, in substance, that this was a dream which showed the relation between the part of her baby-self which was feeling resentful and greedy because of the holiday and because of the recent interferences with times, and that other very envious, tricky part which we had long known to be cat-like, as well as connected with her masturbation phantasies. This cat-part, acting behind her back (serving woman she didn't see), served her a sample of jealousy (jelly! —see!) and immediately shifted her into a masturbation frame of mind (sitting in the prefect's seat, stroking the cat), in projective identification with a big-sister mummy.

Her immediate response, almost explosive, was "Yes, it's like Jane. She's always saying, 'Oh, I heard the most— Oh, no, you wouldn't be interested'. I can't help it, I must hear the rest, even though I know it isn't true. But now I say to her at the end, 'And what is the evidence for that?' like you do with me, and that helps." She resumed her seat at the play table.

Here the push toward motility deriving from her infantile showing off toward the tricky cat-part is clear, and we can see the same internal structure still in the "ape-chase" dream of nine months later where, in fact, the "other girl" who appears to be doing the same thing with the ape is represented as a slightly older girl revealed hiding behind a door just like the serving-woman-behind-her-back in the "sample-of-jelly-see" dream.

If we arrange the patient's stages of cooperation over the four years of analytic work mentioned here they would be roughly as follows:

I Two years of play, characterised by physical activity in the playroom, some toy play, very little drawing, and verbal responses only on inquiry.

II One year of lessened activity, of more drawing and verbalisation, short of dream-analysis.

III Six months—transition to adult technique (as in "sample of jealousy" dream), starting with lying on the couch in the playroom, but unable to control her hands (wall-picking, etc.), her eyes (looking at the analyst) and out-breaks of activity off the couch.

IV Six months—transition to the adult consulting room and full adult technique, and responsibility which became established a few months after her first menstruation and the "grassy bank" dream.

This is the type of sequence which is characteristic—I—spontaneous play, yielding to II—representation in play, drawing and story, yielding to III—dream analysis and IV—"cooperation". The word "cooperation" has been reserved, as you can see, for the "adult" process of responsibility for analytic work, but not because it plays no part in the work with children in the sense of the patient being caught up in the analytic process and working hard within it, as contrasted with wanton attempts to destroy it and break away. It seems better to use a term such as "work" to describe this and to reserve the term "cooperation" for a function closely linked to a sense and acceptance of responsibility. It is of interest, for instance, that with the child described, following the acceptance of the full analytic technique, of "work", a crisis of "cooperation" arose which occupied the next six months of analysis, a virtual stalemate due to her inability to reach a decision about continuing analysis. She was now doing well at school, her social relations with peers was good, her "behaviour" was satisfactory, but her capacity for concern, her ability to love or experience gratitude were all far from established. In other words, her mental pain was "at ebb", as described at the end of Chapter IV. She could have, from her parents' point of view, stopped her analysis, and even some financial considerations might have encouraged her to do so. At this juncture, between outer and inner standards, on the very threshold of the depressive position and the full acknowledgement of psychic reality, she lingered for six unhappy months, including a summer holiday break in which it was left open whether she would continue or not. It was during this separation, in which she found herself crying frequently, feeling lonely, easily hurt and troubled by frightening dreams of an old sort, that her decision to take full responsibility for continuing crystallised. She decided to ask both her parents and the analyst to continue with extremely fruitful results toward a proper "termination" instead of an "interruption" in the "weaning process" (Chapter V).

This taking of responsibility, ultimately responsibility for psychic reality, can occur at an astonishingly early age. I have seen it as early as seven, after only four years of analysis, in a child of unusually vigorous constitution. But this responsibility is, of course, taken by the parents to begin with, when they seek treatment for a child and it is carried by them throughout most of a child-analysis. Even, however, with parents who have themselves been well analysed and whose insight into the child's difficulties is good, this responsibility can only, at best, be of a surrogate sort and must eventually be taken over by the ego of the patient.* In reality the function is early on divided between the parent, who brings the child, pays for the treatment and preserves the child's safety outside analysis, and the analyst who creates and preserves the analytic setting. Eventually all of these functions must be assumed by the ego of the child if self-analysis as a corollary to responsibility for psychic reality is to become established. This includes even the "paying", for the "price" of analysis is not only represented by the fee but is embodied in a far more important way in the pain of the depressive position in internal and external object relations.

* *See* Appendix E.

All this appears to be different in the case of adult neurotic patients who seem to bring themselves, pay for themselves, protect themselves, accept and preserve the setting and to cooperate in every way from the beginning. In borderline and psychotic cases, in the addictions, or with psychopaths, the parallel to child analysis is more obvious, when either the authority or support of some person or institution is required, either constantly or periodically. But closer examination will reveal that the situation is hardly different for all adult patients in qualitative as well as quantitative terms, when correctly viewed from the point of view of psychic structure rather than of mere description.

The central concept for our understanding of the behaviour in analysis of adult patients is acting-out, which must be taken to include acting-out of the unconscious phantasies dominating the transference, both inside and outside the analytical session proper.* More recently a short-hand reference to this distinction has begun to grow up, distinguishing between "acting-in" and "acting-out". The parallel differentiation in the realm of the interpretive aspect of the analytic work takes the form, in the analyst's mind, of the need to decide whether he is going to interpret *content* or *behaviour*. It is well known that a reciprocal relation exists particularly between the patient's ability to bring dreams to the session and these acting-out tendencies. It is an intimate and in no way fortuitous connection which resides in the function of the adult part of the personality in respect to its dominion over, or even, in a sense, possession of, the organ of consciousness. This includes both the capacity for the "observation of psychic qualities" and the control of motility, i.e. behaviour. The "responsibility for psychic reality" involves, within the structure of the mind, functions almost identical to those of an adult supervising the activities of a group of children, namely to observe and, if necessary, to curb their behaviour. In the child material just presented, i.e. in the dream of the "Sewer", this adult function was still delegated to an object, represented as the patient's mother who called her to come up from the sewer and through the door at the left to have her analysis-bath.

* *See* Appendix A.

The child had not yet accepted the responsibility for psychic reality. But a similar situation can be seen in the dream and acting-out of a woman patient at the identical point of development of the analytical process, to whom however a bath had a very different meaning, i.e. of a masturbation chamber, a place of withdrawal. At the beginning of the session, in the sixth year of her analysis, she was complaining about external realities and was attacking the analyst for giving too little heed to the external difficulties in her life— in short, she was behaving in a persecuted and self-pitying way. From the last three years of work we knew very well that these states of mind covered guilt and shame for acting-out or for masturbation and that the content of her complaints represented the solicitude of a bad part of the self which fed her baby parts on the mental equivalent of urine and feces to promote self pity. This part was often represented in dreams as a porter, a bad big sister, a servant or a waiter, giving her dubious food in a dirty restaurant, muddy-looking wine from a broken bottle under the counter, etc.

In the current session these bitter outpourings lasted some forty minutes, during which the facts were revealed one by one, how she had neglected her work, how she had taken a nap when she had meant to write a report for her employer, how she had taken a hot bath because she had began to feel lonely. Finally the dream, not really forgotten but rather shunted aside, emerged. In the dream she was climbing the dome of St. Paul's behind her mother. She was leading by the hand a little girl, who was also herself. But when the child said she felt tired, the patient turned back, leaving her mother, to allow the child to have a nap. And when the child awoke, it was hungry, so she allowed a young woman (who used to work for her sister and was involved in one unhappy love affair after another) to feed her some red stuff (which was the same colour, the patient remarked, as a reddish-brown cow-pat that she had eaten herself in another dream some months earlier).

In this dream and its related acting-out one can see clearly that the negligence of the adult part of the personality is at fault, yielding without struggle to the infantile demands for sensual gratification, regardless of the disruption of her internal

6

(and therefore, in the transference, external) maternal object relationship. Note that we see here both acting-out (the nap, the hot bath, the neglected report) and the acting-in (the persecuted complaints of the unhappy servant-girl part of her infantile structures who feels betrayed and neglected by her lover, the analyst-daddy).

The distinction shown in this dream between object (her mother), adult part (her grown-up self) and infantile parts (the little girl and the servant girl) is not frequently to be found in the dreams of earlier phases of analysis, that is to say, before the threshold of the depressive position (Chapter IV). Instead either the patient is I—a grown-up dealing with other adults, or II—he is a child with other children or adults, or III—he is an adult with children who are specified as not-self, such as his own children.* In the first case we are dealing with dreams in which the adult-self and a child-part-with-the-delusion-of-adulthood (due to massive projective identification) figure. (*See* my paper on the pseudo-mature aspect of character "The Relation of Anal Masturbation and Projective Identification".) In the second case the adult-self has lost its supervisory role while still retaining its capacity to observe psychic qualities, like an inept teacher with a disorderly class of children. In the third case, where the patient is with specific children who are not-self, we deal with situations of projective identification with external objects, where child parts of the personality are permanently or temporarily situated in external objects. A patient's spouse, children or siblings are the most frequent recipients of such projective identifications.

If we consider the dream of this woman patient ("climbing St. Paul's") as type IV, we achieve a sequence of dream types which corresponds to the four types of collaboration seen in child analysis described earlier; I—spontaneous play; II—representational play and verbalisation; III—verbalisation and dream analysis; IV—cooperation and responsibility. We might, for notational purposes, refer to types Ia—IVa, Ic—IVc. The point of this comparison is to show that, for all the superficial differences in behaviour, the actual mode of collaboration in the analytical process is

* *See* Chapter V for expanded discussion.

identical in adults and children, differing only in the forms (not even in the modes) of communication.* A rough correspondence can also be made with the numbered phases of analysis described in Chapters I–IV. The difficulty of doing so, however, resides in the cyclical nature of the transference, explained in earlier chapters, since the over-all sequence of the development of the transference in the total process can also be seen to take place in the smaller time units of analytic work, the session, week, term and year. An instance of this will be demonstrated in the next chapter.

* For further discussion, *see* Chapter VIII.

CHAPTER VII

THE CYCLE OF THE PROCESS IN THE INDIVIDUAL SESSION

It seems likely that the findings presented in this volume came as much from the experience of supervising students and colleagues as from the immediate encounters of the consulting room. A description of the technique of supervision which I employ may help to orientate the reader to the presentations of this chapter. My emphasis is always on the material of the session which I ask supervisees to read to me, commenting and elaborating on their notes freely, stopping the flow as soon as I feel I would have interpreted, usually prior to the supervisee's report of his interpretation. I am in the habit, with new cases, of working without background material, asking initially only the age, sex, number of siblings, marital status, number of children, whether parents are alive, occupation and chief complaint. Of course with cases presented over a period of months a considerable filling-in takes place, but always my emphasis is on the immediacy of the analytic situation, including aspects of the setting, while I leave problems of counter-transference aside as private to the supervisee.

I have found this method congenial with colleagues analysing in other languages and presenting their material in translation, even when their English is extremely limited, provided that the analyst, not his translator, reads the material and I have the typescript before me. This aspect of technique may illustrate the importance of non-verbal communication through the workings of projective and introjective identification that can occur during supervision.

As anxiety and modesty often persuade students to limit their reporting of their interpretive work to an indication of the fact of having ventured an interpretation, I have frequently

66

had the experience of watching the material of the patient develop while lacking detailed knowledge of the content of the interpretive work. The phenomenon of continuity in the unconscious content is equally striking in both adult and child cases, even though the manifest content may change considerably after an interpretation. For this reason, the concept of a "shift" in the material as an indicator of impingement by the interpretive process applies to the latent and not to the manifest content, as will be illustrated in the clinical material to follow.

In order to illustrate and study these factors for teaching purposes, I have also developed a technique for seminars. I will now report from a recent meeting material that serves to introduce the subject of the analytic work as well as to illustrate the analytic cycle in a single session. In a seminar of twelve student and graduate child analysts we have employed the following technique: one member is asked to select in advance a session in the coming week with a patient who is unknown to the seminar leader. It is necessary that this session be followed by an immediate gap in work which would permit a thorough writing-up. This material is duplicated; it contains only the patient's material and a blank space to indicate where interpretations were made. It is distributed *at the seminar* and worked over, without background material. After agreement has been reached as to the formulation of the transference, an assessment is made regarding the evidence of impingement by the interpretive process, breaches of technique and failures of the setting. The actual interpretations are then reviewed, first for their theoretical value and second for their verbal content and style of presentation. The session presented below occupied two ninety-minute seminars on the patient's material and two on the interpretive process. Only the material and seminar formulations will be presented as the content was relatively simple, the interpretations in the main correct from the seminar's point of view, and the principle points of technique and setting adequate.

Jane, 4 years and 6 months, the eldest of two children—with one brother Edward, 2 years. She has come for analysis 5 times a week over the past 18 months.

MATERIAL*   FORMULATION

Patient 1

Wednesday's session—Jane comes in a cowboy suit and hat. On entering the room says that the lady didn't come, she has a cold (the "lady" is an escort arranged to bring her on Wednesday. She was due to start this particular week). Jane goes to a drawer and brings out a green pencil which has a bit of plasticine sticking to it (I do not know whether the plasticine was on the pencil or whether she stuck it on). She makes a gesture of looking for something in the drawer, but not doing it really, she asks me "Where is the red car? I cannot find it. Where have you put it?" With the pencil in her hand she sits at her table and looks at me saying "Your face is red Miss R", then takes the plasticine from the pencil and says it is a rubber. She rubs the table and says it is hard, and, looking at me, says "I won't make a mess today".

She comes dominated by her little boy part (cowboy suit) and immediately seeks out phallic equipment (the green pencil), but is also filled with jealousy and suspicion that the good penis is withheld (the red car) in some secret place inside the analyst (her red face) leaving only a fecal penis for the little boy (the green pencil with the plasticine on it). Hypocrisy, felt to be a fitting revenge for the analyst-mother's deceit, ensues, using the fecal penis (plasticine used as a rubber) to dirty the breast (table).

Interpretation 1

Patient 2

Jane makes a line on the table, starts rubbing it off with the plasticine, dampens the plasticine with saliva and says it needs to have some water. She goes to the jug of water, dampens

The fecal penis and urine, confused with her tongue-penis and saliva, clean the mess on the table-breast, from which she then drinks, in a mood of triumph over the little girl-part

* I am grateful to Miss Ruth Riesenberg for allowing me to use this material.

the plasticine and then drops it into the jug, brings the jug to the table, has a drink from it, takes the plasticine from it and rubs the table with the plasti-- cine. Takes a pencil and makes a line, then a circle, then two lines coming from the circle saying "the legs" and then another two lines saying "the arms". She makes it look from the place she is sitting an up-side down figure; she mentions something about Christine, rubs it off and makes a big J saying "J for Jane".

of herself, projected into Christine, who is upside down, i.e.—confused about tops and bottoms (breasts and buttocks).*

Interpretation 2

Patient 3

She says, showing me the plasti-cine, "My gun, my painting brush" and moves it as if draw-ing with it on the table.

Interpretation 3

The interpretive work has not touched the manic mood as yet but brings the patient into more contact, exhibiting both her creative (paint-brush) and des-tructive (gun) little-boy equip-ment.

Patient 4

Jane smiles saying "This is Edward's suit". "He got it for Christmas." "He hasn't worn it." "I do."

Interpretation 4

The manic mood is touched a bit but defended by denials in respect to the implication of having stolen the brother's masculinity (it isn't really his but was given him, and only so recently, and besides it doesn't fit him and anyhow he doesn't care about it).

* *See* Appendix J.

Patient 5

Jane drops the plasticine into the water saying "Plop", brings a towel, covers the jug with the towel and says "A flower will grow there", gives me a very seductive smile, wraps the towel around the jug and says "It makes it nice and warm".

Faced with the eroding effect of the interpretation on her manic situation, Jane begins to seduce the analyst to connive in the mania, offering her (mummy) a baby (flower), but the "Plop" betrays the fecal nature of the impregnation of the tummy (jug).

Interpretation 5

Patient 6

She takes the towel off the jug and says "A fish"; picking the plasticine out of it she says "No —a flower—but it is growing".

Interpretation 6

Having failed in her offer of a girl baby (flower), she now promises a boy (fish) but without conviction, returning to the hope that the girl (flower) may still grow. She is beginning to show and feel some anxiety now as her manic reparativeness crumbles.

Patient 7

She puts the towel back on the jug and starts moving the jug, tipping it, then water starts coming out of it wetting the towel. Some water wets her cowboy trousers. She says "It is wet", goes to a chair where the towel usually is; realising then that the towel is on the jug and is wet, ·she says "I'll have to take off my cowboy suit and put it to dry", proceeding to do so, and putting the trousers on the fire fence; she comes back to the water, ends by spilling it all on the floor, and throws the jug away.

The mania is shattered, not only by the impossibility of the representation (as when children attempt acts beyond their competence) but brought about by Jane (tipping the jug) acknowledging that she has been idealising her urination and defecation into the toilet-mummy and is in dread of her products not being contained (the toilet overflowing, the analyst losing patience, etc.), splitting off again her masculinity once more into the baby-brother-at-the-breast (the cowboy-suit before the fire). Her femininity immediately

She looks at her shoes, points out that they are wet, puts more water on them, and says "My hushpuppies". "They are no good. They won't be of any use no more."

takes the stage, messing the breasts (her shoes, the Hushpuppies), and feeling hopeless.

Interpretation 7

Patient 8

Jane is looking with a half distressed expression on her face, says "Ha!" "I don't care." "Ha!"

She is delicately poised between the pain of the hopelessness and abandoning herself to despair ("I don't care"). *CRISIS I.*

Interpretation 8

Patient 9

She says "I hate you." "You are horrible." "You are all messed." "You made it all this wet." "I really do hate you." "I really do." "And anyhow I don't care."

This interpretation seems to have tipped the balance toward abandoning herself, which commences with a mixture of accusation and slander against the analyst-mummy that shows the first clear differentiation of external (transference) and internal (the situation of her masturbation phantasies and dreams represented in the earlier play). In effect she says now, "It is because I hate you, analyst-mother, when you talk to me that way (Interpretation 8) that I do such horrible things to my internal mummy-breasts (Hushpuppies)."

Interpretation 9

Patient 10

Half singing and half saying it she says "It's raining, it's pouring".

Mockery of the damaged mother who has been wet and soiled, but whose husband is too lazy

Interpretation 10

to repair her ("The old man is snoring", etc.). This is the first oedipal material in this session, resulting from her giving up the manic denial of the distinction between adults and children in favour of a narcissistic self-abandonment.

Patient 11

Jane says "I want to go to toilet"; she picks up a little wooden house, wets it in the water on the floor and says "It's chimney is coming down".

Interpretation 11

The toilet-wish here combines the desire to expel her internal situation, with the desire to go into the toilet herself like the upside-down Christine, along with her crumbling and ruined objects (chimney, Hush-puppies).

Patient 12

She lies down on the couch, says "I don't care", picks her nose and eats the pickings. Takes a doll from the drawer, says "It's Helen" (mother's name). "It's Miss R" (analyst). "I will eat up her bumper." She tries to pull off doll's skirt and says "I want her knickers off." "I want to take them off."

Interpretation 12

The full abandonment to anal preoccupations emerges with the nose picking and other indications of equating breasts with buttocks, her bottom with the mummy's, and of idealising her feces as food—i.e.—having thrown *herself* into the toilet to revel in anal perversity. She is relatively out of contact again, not with the analyst and analytic situation, but with the interpretive process.

Patient 13

Jane tries to push the doll's leg inside the keyholes of several drawers, saying "Clump—clump —a tiger." "Ha!" "Clump—clump—a crocodile." "Ha!" "Eating it up."

The keyhole, representing her voyeurism, now becomes manifestly orally sadistic, like a tiger or crocodile, attacking the analyst-mother's breasts represented by the doll's feet, linked

Interpretation 13

to the spoiled Hushpuppies. This probably implies getting inside the mother with the eyes and eating the inside of the breast-buttocks.

Patient 14

Jane laughs, takes out two flannels from the drawer, puts them on the couch, then takes a tissue hankie from the drawer; while doing this she is singing "Poo Poo" several times. Says "Ha!" "I'll bring the mice, they are squeeky"; she comes to me and gets her hand into my pocket with the same kind of noises of "Aha!" "Aha!" Takes a tissue out of my pocket saying "Aha!" "Anyhow." She goes back to the couch tearing the hankie into bits and dropping them onto the floor. (While I am interpreting she is picking her nose and eating the pickings.)

This theme becomes even clearer now, as the mice-bits of herself get into the analyst-mother's pockets, also represented by the two flannels, aiming to destroy the good tissues (idealised feces of the mother), then tearing them to bits to form mouse-feces. All this is done in manic triumph, combining voyeurism, anal and oral sadism.

Interpretation 14

Patient 15

Jane goes back to the flannel on the couch saying "I will make lovely pancakes." "None for you." "None for mummy." "All for me."

Interpretation 15

Having emptied the mother of her idealised feces, the child turns to feeding herself with her own idealised mouse-feces, reversing the situation in which the mother is suspected of keeping all the good food for herself and her inside babies and little-brother-at-the-breast, still represented by the cowboy-suit-before-the-fire.

Patient 16

She looks rather provocative, takes a bit of paper, saying "It is my chewing-gum". "Lovely pancakes." This goes on for a while; meanwhile she is rolling and folding the flannels.

Interpretation 16

More in contact with the analyst, pressing to continue the failing manic triumph, as the pancakes begin to alter into chewing-gum, delicately balanced between being a delicious chewy substance and a sticky mess.

Patient 17

Jane says "I don't know and I don't care." And again with the same melody singing "It's raining, it's pouring." She is looking half worried and half provocative with a very curious expression of a struggle going on in her.

Interpretation 17

The interpretive process is reaching her again and the delicate balance between persecutory and depressive anxieties returns, along with the despairing denial of psychic reality ("I don't care") and the contempt for the father ("It's raining, it's pouring", etc.), as at Patient 10. *CRISIS II.*

Patient 18

Jane says "Ha!" "Ha!" "Anyhow, I'm having a drink from the rain." "I want to go to the toilet."

Interpretation 18

The balance continues, with new evidence of depressive pressure ("having a drink from the rain" equals drinking-my-tears), but without conviction in her mania.

Patient 19

Jane speaks about school, says that she wants a badge, that Mrs. King has a Budgy, "A dicky-bird you know, not Father Christmas's dicky-bird; she has two, one at home and one in the front room."

The depression wins through and the child's more adult function, of talking to the analyst about school, becomes a vehicle for the expression of infantile misery, yearning for nipples of her own (the badge)

Interpretation 19

on the one hand, and for the mother's (the teacher's two dicky-birds, differentiated from the father's penis, Father Christmas's dicky-bird). This is the first "cooperation" as distinct from "acting-in".

Patient 20

Jane says "Oh! Mrs. King has lots and lots of dicky-birds and lots and lots of children"; she speaks at some length about this.

In this depressed and thoughtful mood confusion between the outside (dicky-bird nipples) and the inside (lots of children) of the mother's rich body emerges.

Interpretation 20

Patient 21

Jane is lying down quietly on the couch, mumbles something about Mrs. King and starts singing "The London bridge is falling down—is falling down—my fair lady." All this with a sad voice and repeated 3 or 4 times.

The depressive feeling about the destruction of the nipples comes out in a sad chant, linking back to the chimney material (Patient 11), possibly emphasising the beauty of the breast ("My fair lady").

Interpretation 21

Patient 22

Jane is very serious and with an expression on her face as though a struggle is going on in her and says "The London bridge."

Interpretation 22

This toleration of depressive pain has lasted probably five minutes now, physically in contact with the couch at an infantile level, needing to be cuddled, but held also by the analyst's voice. At the same time she seems in good intellectual contact with the content of the analyst's interpretations.

Patient 23

Jane starts saying "Oh!" "I", here changes her voice and says "I don't care." "It wins."	Probably sensing the winding-up quality in the analyst's voice, the child breaks with the depressive pain.

Interpretation 23

Patient 24

It is the end of the session and I have to tidy. Jane walks to my arm chair, points at the pattern of the cover and says "The fox", "The fox that eats all the chicks out", "I win", "The fox."	The oral-sadism triumphs, the "fox" part of herself, inside the analyst-mother (in the pattern on the chair that is visualised, not actually represented) eating up the rival babies and the inside of the breasts (chicks).

As I have said earlier, when the seminar turned its attention to the interpretive work of the analyst, it was found to be fundamentally correct in respect of geography, distribution of parts of the self, nature of the objects and the mechanisms employed. Only one defect could be found which may have affected the course of the transference process. At Interpretation 8 the analyst introduced the idea of "littleness", which seems not to have been central in the material. It may have precipitated the spiteful *tu quoque* type of attack at Patient 9 and facilitated the child's escape from the depressive anxiety at CRISIS I.

This material will be used in Chapter VIII as a reference point for discussion of the analytic work. Before turning to that central task, it might be of interest to note the faithfulness with which the flow of an individual session can represent, and thus contain, the basic scheme of the analytic process.

(1) From Patient 1 through 6 Jane's play is pure acting-in the transference, dominated by massive projective identification, via her little brother and his cowboy suit, with the father's reparative and creative penis. (*See* Chapter II.)

(2) Patient 7 through 16 Jane's play moves into more contact with the analyst mother, zonal confusions are central and projective identification phantasies involve more intrusive

raids on the mother's contents and less the appropriation of her identity. (*See* Chapter III.)

(3) From Patient 17 through 22 the zonal confusions have been set aside, the abandonment to despair and sadism overcome, and an approach to the feeding breasts and nipples, rife with depressive pain (CRISIS II), takes the stage (*see* Chapter IV); only to break under the impact of the approaching end of the session. It is only in this area of the material that differentiation of external and internal reality is apparent.

CHAPTER VIII

THE ANALYTICAL WORK

ONE cannot suppose that material such as that in Chapter VII can be convincing in regard to details of the formulation, yet it is illustrative of the modes of thought and methods of work in the group whereby the in-breeding of thought and expression give rise to a homogeneity of outlook which cannot avoid being idiosyncratic in its superficial aspects. But it will be seen to illustrate the points which we must now examine in detail in our investigation of the nature of the analytic work.

In a certain sense all of this book is dedicated to the thesis that the major work of analysis is done in the unconscious of the patient whence the "natural history" of the analytic process emanates. The analyst's contribution, on the other hand, is of two sorts, the creation and maintenance of the setting within which the analytic process, the evolution of the transference, can take place, and secondly in creating that aspect of the interpretive process which at various points facilitates the passing of certain obstacles to this evolution as well as, by the building up of insight, bulwarks the personality of the patient against regression. As these two functions appear to be fundamentally distinct, they may usefully be dealt with separately in terms of (*a*) the *setting* and (*b*) the *working through*.

THE SETTING

The fundamentals of analytic technique were made explicit by Freud, and have changed little since, particularly in the series of technical papers before World War I. There is no need to review them here. The gradual evolution, or one might say, the purification, of the method has come about so that psycho-analysis is now a clearly distinguishable process in its technique from psycho-therapies which employ such diverse elements as environmental-manipulation, advice, education, encouragement, drugs, milieu therapy, persuasion, suggestion, hypnosis, religious conversion, occupational therapy, group experience, hormonal treatments, cosmetic or plastic surgical alteration, etc. These methods we need not discuss. Similarly the clarification of the requirement of sequestration for the process has become steadily and generally apparent, so that we recognise the incompatibility of analysis with extra-mural social relations with the patient, the hazard imposed by pre-analytic social contact, the intrusive effect on patients of information about the analyst's way of life, politics, aesthetic preferences, non-analytic interests and health. With more psychotic patients it is clear that even treatment in a consulting room in the analyst's home may prove to be intolerable. The delicacy of the financial situation, the time arrangements and the formal aspects of the setting are also widely known and accepted. We can with some certainty discriminate now between technique and style, realising that this latter variable amongst analysts is neither avoidable nor interfering as regards findings and scientific communication. None of these well-established aspects of the setting need occupy us here.

Instead we must turn our attention to the fundamental unit of the setting, the state of mind of the analyst, and explore the various aspects that are embodied in the concept, the *psycho-analytic attitude.*

All that has been written in this book proclaims that the foundation of this attitude must be *dedication to the psycho-analytic method.* It is incompatible with the fundamental conception of the transference to consider that any aspect of the benefit that patients receive from psycho-analysis should arise as an emanation from any qualities of the person of the analyst other than his analytic functions, i.e.—his presiding over the psycho-analytic process.

In corollary to this dedication, the analytic attitude implies a *commitment to the patient* to do the best analytic work of which he, the analyst, is capable and to pursue it as long as he has hope, substantiated by evidence, that the patient is *progressing in his personality structure* or has reached a point of self-analytic capacity which gives promise of his being able to preserve and extend his gains without the help of regular sessions with his analyst.

"Doing his best analytic work" signifies that the analyst undertakes to set aside a certain "time of his life" for an indefinite period within which he intends to pursue the psycho-analytic method, with no consideration of sacrifice in mental pain to himself, to the limit of his toleration, and within a framework of consideration for the patient's and his own physical safety. But this means also that the analyst undertakes to protect others than himself from having any sacrifice imposed upon them for the patient's sake, especially the families involved, analyst's and patient's. This is of special importance for the development of the analyst's attitude toward acting-out, payment, extra sessions, phone calls, hospitalisation, the management of suicidal dangers and aggressive behaviour.

The focal point is, of course, the analyst's undertaking to bear, to the limit of his capacity, the full brunt of the patient's projections of mental pain, employing only his supervisor and, if still under treatment, his own analyst to augment his capacities in this regard. Such a conception is not meant to imply anything in the least heroic and is felt to be absolutely in the best tradition of medical ethics. It must be recognised, therefore, that an analyst's *inner qualification* for independent work is a very different matter from his external qualification, bestowed by his Institute and Society, to represent himself to the world as a psycho-analyst. Indeed the question may reasonably be raised whether an analyst would *ever* wish to work independently of colleagues, without any supervision for his most difficult cases, without the regular experience of seminars or study groups that stem the drift, induced by the constant pressure of patients upon his counter-transference, away from the psycho-analytic method and toward a megalomanic exercise of unique therapeutic power.

It is a matter of some urgent consideration to decide what is the analyst's proper attitude in regard to the "therapy" and the "benefit" that the analytic work is meant to make available to his patient. Certainly from the ethical point of view he is bound in contract with his patient to strive to benefit him by means of the analytic method, and, by the medical ethic of *nihil nocere*, to do him no harm. Yet as surely as in the case of surgery, psycho-analytic treatment cannot be without danger to the patient, both mentally and physically. Common sense would suggest that therapeutic zeal, an urgent desire to bring benefit to a patient, would be as beneficial a quality in an analyst as in a physician or surgeon. But analytic insight shows clearly that this is far from true. Therapeutic zeal contains many severe and hidden pitfalls for psycho-analytic work, the most important being the following factor. While in medical care trust by the patient needs to take the form of submission to his doctor's judgement and willingness to follow his regimen, trust is not a requirement of analytic work. Indeed it is impossible at the outset and can only grow gradually from fruitful years of experience of the analytic process.* The passivity of medical trust is a transference state acted out with childlike submission to a parental figure. Freud's earliest experience of hypnosis shows him how limited such a method necessarily was. Child-like trust, like its extension in the submission to hypnosis, we now know to involve a process of splitting and projective identification in which the *adult* part of the personality is temporarily made over to the physician.

This does in fact occur, despite all technical precautions, with psychotic patients and to some degree in the earlier phases of analysis with all patients. But, should it continue, it would draw a line against progress into the depressive position. Such a projection of all, or part, of the adult segment of the personality into the analyst intensifies the dependence which is in any case intense, especially when the feeding-breast relationship is approached. (*See* Chapter IV.) It intensifies this dependence on the analytic process by attaching it to the person of the analyst in a most tenacious way. This "sticky" transference, in which the analyst, rather than the process and the internal objects, is felt to be unique, manifests itself by a most intense pressure on the counter-transference of the analyst. While insight and maturity may protect him from being swept into a megalomanic state, an insidious megalomania with respect to the particular patient can none-theless arise and escape notice. Its form is always therapeutic

* *See* Chapter IV and Appendix I.

zeal—its hallmark the interminable analysis—its background the unverbalised and unrecognised threat of suicide.

But even in a milder form, the therapeutic zeal of the analyst induces a splitting off and projection of aspects of the patient's adult personality involving initiative, a quest for self-esteem, a desire to "pull his weight". It is vitiating and conducive to inertia, especially since the dread of termination hangs in the air as soon as the experience of the dependence on the feeding breast has been acknowledged.

What is to sustain the analyst, other than his need to earn a living, if a curtailment of therapeutic zeal is required, while the analytic attitude necessitates the acceptance of projections of mental pain? "Devotion to the analytic method" surely cannot imply a rich enough reward to balance that pain. Perhaps the answer is scientific curiosity. It may turn out, after all, that there are better ways of making a living and better ways of relieving suffering than by the practice of psycho-analysis by the full, uncompromising method. I have suggested earlier that psycho-analysis proper is moving away from its original position as a sub-speciality of psychological medicine into a place, somewhere within the triangle between medicine, education and child rearing—at once a research science and a training ground for other disciplines. My own experience leads me to believe that these two factors, scientific curiosity and devotion to method, reinforce one another, potentiate one another, to produce a strength of determination which is far greater than could be expected from a mere addition of the two factors. We know that, acting separately, on the form of loyalty to teachers and a thirst for knowledge, these two qualities of character promote restriction of the scientific thought and wild experimentation respectively. Acting to-gether, in integration within the depressive position, they greatly increase the tolerance to the incidental pain attending the method of investigation.

The question now arises whether the interpretive activity of the analyst is to be understood as exercised entirely in the service of the "working through" aspect of the work or whether also in some way as part of the setting. It is clear that the task of the analytic attitude involves several elements: to receive the material, content and behaviour; to contain the projection of mental pain; to think about the transference situation; and finally to communicate the analyst's under-standing, be it ever so tentative, from moment to moment. If we return to Jane's material studied by the seminar, we can see that a crisis of depressive pain arose twice, once after Interpretation 11 and next after Interpretation 18, in both cases centering on her wish to "go to the toilet". Both of these interpretations were substantially correct, differing only in a greater emphasis in Interpretation 18 on the underlying depressive anxieties which were being defended against, by "going to the toilet" in order to throw away both her damaged objects and herself. Clearly Interpretation 11 has not modified the situation and is followed by abandonment to anal sadism. Interpretation 18 has produced a shift toward the acceptance of depressive anxiety, promoting the "dicky-bird" material and failing only as the end of the hour approached.

It would of course be absurd to suggest that the other interpretive work has been futile and Interpretation 18 unique, especially as the content is in no way special, nor more accurate. Clearly what has altered is the child's availability to the *content* of the interpretation. Fluctuations in her contact can be seen in the material: from being entirely absorbed in the acting in the transference of her internal relations she moves into a position of responsiveness to the analyst, as at Patient 3 through 6, losing it again at Patient 7 and 8, recovering at Patient 9, etc.

This "getting through" of the interpretive activity disrupted the "acting-in" aspect of the material and reestablishes analytic "work" by the patient, based on a differentiation of external from internal reality. But only at Patient 19 has "cooperation" been momentarily achieved, to be shattered a few minutes later as the end of the session approached.

I would suggest that the aspect of the interpretive work that breaks through the *acting-in* may most fruitfully be taken as part of the "setting" of the analytic process; it is effective in the continual declaration of the analytic attitude as follows: "I am your analyst, an external figure; I receive but am not dominated by your projections; I am still able to think for myself; I am still able to communicate my thoughts to you." It is true that there are times with children who are being excessively destructive, or with psychotic adults who are threatening assault, when the ultimate act of individuality, the premature ending of a session, must be invoked to refute claims of omnipotent control. But the analyst mainly relies on the *fact* that he is still able to think and interpret in order to accomplish this clarification.

This conclusion points to the fact that there is a function of interpretation related to the analyst's struggles to preserve the analytic attitude rather than to the accuracy with which he is able to comprehend the unconscious meaning of the material. In a sense the outcome may be said to depend primarily, for its success, on how *hard* the analyst works, rather than on his talent or experience. It explains why some workers are able to produce more movement with patients as students than later in their careers; why the thrill of learning has such a vitalising effect on the process; why a little supervision which supports the analyst's tolerance to the projections can bring a stalled process to life again; why the quest for scientific knowledge can enable an analyst to persevere with patients who continually project despair.

Conversely silence in the analyst will always produce increased anxiety and regression in the patient, and a general falling off of the analyst's interpretive activity promotes acting-out.

THE TWO LEVELS OF WORKING THROUGH

"One must allow the patient to become more conversant with this resistance with which he has now become acquainted, to *work through* it, to overcome it, by continuing, in defiance of it, the analytical work according to the fundamental role of analysis. Only when the resistance is at its height can the analyst, working in common with his patient, discover the repressed instinctual impulses which are feeding the resistance; and it is this kind of experience which convinces the patient of the existence and power of such impulses. The doctor has nothing else to do than to wait and let things take their course, a course which cannot be avoided nor always hastened. If he holds fast to this conviction he will often be spared the illusion of having failed when in fact he is conducting the treatment on the right lines."* With these words Freud, in his 1914 paper "Remembering, Repeating and Working Through" introduced this momentous concept to psycho-analysis, and with a sweep which seems hardly to leave any-thing unsaid. But when he took up the concept again in 1926 in the addenda to "Inhibitions, Symptoms and Anxiety", his views had become more structural, locating resistance primarily in the ego, but well aware that "even after the ego has decided to relinquish its resistances it still has difficulty in undoing the repression".† It is the view implied in this book that the function of "decid(ing) to relinquish" the resistances corresponds to insight and commitment to responsi-bility for psychic reality by the adult part of the personality, while the "undoing of the repressions" corresponds to struc-tural, dynamic and economic change at the infantile levels.

I have already expressed the view that one function of the content of the interpretive process is to build up insight in the adult part in order that these "decis(ions) to relinquish" may be made and sustained as bulwarks against regression. I wish now to turn attention first to its other function, the facilitation of working through by means of the modification of anxiety.

There can be no possibility of discussing the analytic method without referring each point to a conception of the mental apparatus. I think that the one implied in this book stresses structure above the other categories of metapsychological study. Melanie Klein followed Freud closely in her very concrete conception of internal objects. In the structural sense such objects are seen possessed of a portion of the mental apparatus, with all its inherent capacities, even the ability to seize control of the organ of consciousness (as in demoniacal possession, hypnosis and certain types of *folie a deux*). Integration, and conversely dis-integration, of self and internal objects always move in parallel rather than in series.‡ The internal objects, in the course of development, change slowly from an assortment of part-objects with primarily superego functions (prohibitive and inhibitive) toward a combined-parent-figure with primarily ego-ideal functions (inspirational).

* S.E. 20, page 159.
† S.E. 12, page 155.
‡ *See* Appendix J.

The sense of identity which comes from the experience of introjective identification contains always a gradient composed of depressive unworthiness and inferiority feelings, urging further development. The delusion of identity due to projective identification on the other hand contains a sense of accomplished fact, built-in smugness, so to speak.

If the sequence of events in the natural history of the psycho-analytic process is as faithful a recapitulation of early development as I am suggesting, we can see that the progress from superego to ego ideal is first and foremost a consequence of the surrendering of omnipotence by the infantile parts of the self. One may suppose that, extrapolated, this process would approach asymptomatically to a state of "giving them (the internal parents) their freedom", meaning freedom to preside over the infantile structures, and therefore over the unconscious.

The crucial step in this direction, the "threshold of the depressive position", is described in Chapter IV. It involves both of Freud's descriptions, the "decis(ion) to oppose the resistances" and the "working through of the resistances". . . . The former, as I have said, is viewed here as a function of the adult part of the personality, equivalent to a contract, vow, or commitment, while the latter is a slow and tedious process of bit-by-bit surrendering of the omnipotence (and therefore, necessarily, of the masturbatory practices which generate it)* at infantile levels. The point that I wish to make by this diversion into theory is that: modification of anxiety is shown in unconscious phantasy by *alterations in psychic structure* on the one hand and *changes in the level of omnipotence* on the other. This is just as true of the defensive measures adopted by the ego as it is of the therapeutic influence of the interpretations which struggle against them. Any other alteration of the anxiety is transient and is spoken of here as "modulation" rather than "modification".

If we turn back to Jane's material in Chapter VII, it becomes apparent that the interpretive process, consisting of some twenty-four interpretations in the one session, has functioned first and foremost as part of the setting for the

---

* *See* Appendices F and G.

unfolding of the child's object relations. Until Patient 4 she was virtually out of contact with the analyst as an external person. Thereafter her contact was infantile until Crisis I with its brief outbreak of hatred, and became "adult" only for the brief depressive period after Crisis II. We may say that the contribution of the interpretive process to the working through seems only clearly to have taken place at Interpretation 18, having failed at Interpretation 8, perhaps because of the redundant theme of "littleness". All the interpretations were of an "immediate" sort, dealing with the moment-to-moment transference process.

If we compare this with the "Samples of Jelly-see" dream and the consequences of its interpretation, in which old patterns were worked over in a new form and links to past material were established, we see a difference. Insight has begun to take shape in the adult-part of the personality, represented in the child's "What's the evidence, I say to her" association. This child had begun to learn how to deal with the omniscience and omnipotence of the destructive part of her infantile organisation, as a bulwark against the regression shown in the dream (the shift to the prefect's seat, stroking the cat).

The type of insight which enables a patient such as this child to alter her relationship to external figures seems often to represent an identification with an external figure based, we would have to suspect, either on mimicry or on projective identification (they may in fact really be the same thing). If the child asks her friend, "What's the evidence?" as the analyst has asked her many times in the past, we can only guess at the mental dynamics and structures that are operative. To find the answer to this we must study the transference, especially as it is revealed through dreams. What we wish to know is how the content of interpretation alters the internal organisation of objects, as well as infantile and adult parts of the self. My experience has led me to the conclusion that insight, conveyed by interpretations, lodges in two ways in the mental apparatus, first of all as *new equipment for the internal objects* and secondly as *new equipment for the adult self*. I call it equipment to distinguish it from the qualities of goodness and badness in their many forms that are indissolubly bound

up with the structure brought about by splitting-and-idealisation which cannot be good, but only idealised in the sense
that it has been divested of all badness. In fact we see over
and over that such objects are extremely persecuting in their
perfection and consequent perfectionist demands.

I mean by equipment something essentially *useful*, a *content*
of mind rather than a *quality* of mind. Objects may, by
integration, become as good and as strong as the structures
of the self will allow, and this also seems to mean as beautiful
as is allowed.* But the goodness, strength and beauty of
objects are not essentially *useful*, although the love they
engender has far-reaching implications for the personality as
a whole. In addition to these qualities the objects must have
knowledge, skills, wisdom, the form and content of which
must necessarily be a reflection of the external culture, of
which the science of psycho-analysis has become a part.

While the introjective activity at the breast (Chapter IV)
in the analytic process, through its archaic significance,
produces the quality of the objects, it is the interpretive
process, I suggest, that alters the equipment of the internal
objects and thus, through introjective identification, gradually
of the adult part of the self ("But now I say to her, etc.").
Some material may illustrate this point and make it more
vivid.

A pubertal girl who had had a long and arduous analysis
for severe schizoid difficulties found herself becoming manically
excited as a holiday approached. She knew well its dangers
since in the previous year on the occasion of her first holiday
away from the family, she had been quite swept away by it,
the consequence being a recrudescence of her most distressing
symptoms followed by loss of a whole term of analytic work
spent in regaining the lost ground. In the following two
terms of analysis she had worked as never before and made a
substantial intrusion into the depressive position. This had
brought not only a degree of symptom relief which quite
astonished her but a totally unexpected devotion to the
analysis that for years she had consciously despised.

Exams past, festivities afoot, and another holiday away
from the family approaching, a manic excitement seized her

* *See* Appendix L.

and, despite her worry and struggle, produced sessions of flippant, chatty contempt which finally had to be dealt with very firmly, even harshly, by a technique that caricatured her infantile structures. I only used this technique in extremity with this patient, due to her exquisite sensitivity to anything savouring of ridicule, she herself being a wanton virtuoso of the art.

That night she dreamed that she was at prayers in school, led by the headmistress, singing a hymn, all the girls kneeling. Next to her was a girl named Gay whom she hardly knew. This girl was in such a state of infectious hilarity that the patient herself could hardly keep from laughing. When the headmistress stopped the hymn and scolded the girl, Gay cheeked her outrageously in reply. When the headmistress threatened her for this disrespect, the girl denied that it was she and pointed to the patient, who suddenly felt very frightened and unable to defend herself. But the head-mistress went behind a curtain and brought out a tape recorder which she slipped into a slot in the podium where it fitted perfectly. As soon as she played back the tape, the patient ceased to feel either afraid or excited since the identity of the culprit was unmistakably revealed.

In this dream we see that the internal mother has acquired a piece of equipment by which the splitting in the patient can be clarified, bringing good parts into alliance with good objects and thus preventing the bad part from being dominant in her personality structure (the manic wave). This has "modified" her anxiety.

The holiday went well, to her great relief and delight, for she had been able to maintain herself with good sense and good spirits throughout some severe temptations and some frightening dislocations. The first two days of subsequent analytic work dealt with the events of her trip, including visits to some caves and a boys' school. These events had disturbed her very much in two areas of phantasy, namely her confusion between the inside and outside of her objects on the one hand and her confusion between vagina and rectum on the other.

The night of the second session she had two dreams. In the first it was Sunday and her parents were away, leaving her with a friend who suggested that they should take a ride in the car. This they did, in a huge open van, the friend driving wildly on the wrong side of the road while the patient lay in the back, until they ended up half on the verge with the car on its side. As another car was approaching rapidly and was about to crash into them, she had to jump out and, grasping the rear of the car, she dragged it out of the way.

From abundant earlier material I could interpret to her, with her full agreement, that this was a dream of her manic state of mind, caused by the delinquent sexual activities and masturbation of her infantile structures, now, as in early life, with one hand in front (the friend driving) as she urinated and the other grasping her bottom to spread her buttocks (the van) as she defecated in her cot. The oncoming car represented the dangerous feces rushing from her bottom. It was all clearly a revenge against the going-away analyst-parents.

She then related the second dream, which, while it appeared to be a continuation of the first, seemed to take place on the following Sunday. Again her parents were away and again she was alone with her friend who again suggested that they should take a ride. The patient refused and went downstairs where at first there seemed to be a lot of people. Then they had gone and she seemed to have in her hand four pink postcards, addressed to someone she had never heard of, named M. T. Brown.

Clearly, instead of masturbating and soiling her cot in revenge against the parents as a baby, her dream was now dominated by a more adult part which was able to toilet herself, the feces being represented by the crowd of people who disappear, and to clean herself. The four fingers covered with pink toilet tissue were represented by the four postcards and directed to her empty rectum (M. T. Brown).

Before the holiday, then, she was in danger of being swept away on the manic wave, dominated by the destructive part of herself, by the girl who laughed at prayers and cheeked the headmistress. At that time the activities of the external object, the analyst, were required to reestablish the equipment of her internal object, represented by the headmistress and her tape recorder. After the holiday she was able, even in the depths of sleep, to wrest back the control of her organisation, showing in the second dream the identification in her adult self with the analyst-mother, for, while the postcards represent fingers holding toilet tissue, they must also represent verbal messages. Her bottom has been cleaned by insight!

To recapitulate then, I am suggesting that the working through aspect of the analytic process, which permits movement forward in the transference from one phase to another and finally to termination and self-analysis—that this aspect, unlike those other facets of the analytic work, which contribute to the maintenance of the setting, rests upon the effect of the *content* of the interpretations. I have cited some clinical material to illustrate how the content of interpretation lodges as new "equipment" in internal objects, enabling them to modify infantile structure and curb infantile omnipotence. It is on the basis of an introjective identification with the newly "equipped" object that the adult part of the personality improves its capacity for control over infantile structures and thus of acting-out. This improved insight by way of introjective identification can be distinguished from mere intellectual insight.

CHAPTER IX

PSYCHO-ANALYSIS AS A HUMAN ACTIVITY*

FREUD's early sanguine assumption that anyone who could learn to analyse his own dreams could practise analysis has progressed to its own antipodes. We now must ask the serious question how anyone can practise analysis without being damaged. Of course every occupation has its special hazards, so no complaint is allowable. Rather it is necessary to look with a sober glance at the hazards of psycho-analytic work, construe and test the safety measures and prophylactic schemes.

No doubt in its own way the so called training analysis has been the bastion of self-defence of the analyst against the rigours of analytic work and will continue to be so, most realistically when it is continued in a systematic way as a self-analysis. The second rampart has been the analytic method, the faithful pursuit of which has been the psycho-analyst's best defence against being lured into ambush of counter-transference activites, the harbinger of which is almost always the breach in technique.

Probably neither of these preparatory schemes can continue to function effectively for the practising analyst without the scientific society of other analysts, at seminars and scientific meetings, supervisions and congresses. The history of analysis in the future is not likely to include the lone pioneer bringing this discipline to new areas of the earth. It will almost certainly be possible only as group efforts. What part the published literature plays in all this is still, I believe, obscure. Certainly only the intellectual outlines of a scientific advance in our

* Previously published in *Revista Uruguaya di Psicoanalisis Tomo VII*, No. 4, p. 373, 1965.

field is communicable in writing, except to the rare individual with first-rate literary talent, such as Freud.

Now, I mention all these well-known aspects of the problem in order to set them aside and focus attention on a more individual and personal level of the predicament: the practice of psycho-analysis as an act of virtuosity, a combination of artistic and athletic activity. Here the term "condition" becomes as applicable to the psycho-analyst as to the race-horse, although its substance needs elucidation. This I think is the term central to this chapter, not the skill, nor the knowledge, nor the character of the psycho-analyst, but his "condition", and how to stay *in* it, rather than falling *out* of it.

Just as an athlete's condition has a background in training and a violinist's a background in practice, so an analyst's "condition" has a background in a daily, weekly, term-wise and yearly scheme of activities which are calculated to be in direct and immediate support of his analytic performance. I could name some of the areas which require modulation. For instance: the number of hours of work, the amount of money he earns, the distribution of types and severity of illness in his patients, the amount of rest between patients, the amount of note-writing and note-reading before and after patients, the extent of participation in post-graduate education, the amount of reading of the literature, of writing papers, of lecturing or teaching—of holiday. The list of course could be expanded, but for each item in the supporting structure the analyst must find and maintain an optimum, being prepared to alter it when evidence demands, and to resist its alteration in the face of external demands.

In all such considerations there must be a guiding principle. The aim is stability, the secret is simplicity, but the guiding principle, I suggest, should be "strain", balanced but close to the limit. A colleague reported to me that her son, when chided for his many rugger bruises, replied that "if it didn't hurt it wasn't sport". I have referred to psycho-analytic activity as a mixture of artistic and athletic effort perhaps because of this central fact, that to be done well it must "hurt". It must be done under great strain, approaching the analyst's limit. Only on a background of work-under-balanced-strain can there emerge that mysterious function of creativity, which alone enables a worker to feel he has a place in a scientific fellowship of peers, rather than in a guild of masters, journeymen and apprentices. The problem is a social one as well, for the preservation of scientific individuality and avoidance of enervating isolation is no easy task, where "schools" and "groups" abound. But the social and individual problems are very closely linked, as my list suggests.

The reason that psycho-analytic *activity* may be placed on a footing with those of the virtuoso and the athlete is because they all rely absolutely, in the heat of the performance, upon the unconscious, rallied and observed by the organ of consciousness. It is fortunate that psycho-analysis tends to impose regularity, although perhaps too few analysts take advantage of this by keeping their schedules in order, the same patient seen at the same time each day, occasional professional activities such as lectures and meetings left for the evening, etc. It is noticeable that the quality of work later during a day is adversely affected when a patient or student cancels, even in advance, leaving a gap in the day's work. Welcome as the relaxation may be, or useful as the time may prove for other activities, it breaks up the "pace" of the work.

When it is recognised how exacting analytic work is, how "off" days can impede the deepening of the transference in the earlier phases and pose obstacles to the working through later on, the need of planning to maintain "pace" and "condition" stands forth clearly. Seeing a patient through the "threshold" into the depressive position at infantile levels of the personality is certainly the crucial step in establishing the basis of stability of personality structure, just as overcoming massive projective identification is crucial in establishing the basis of mental health, free from psychosis.* But penetration through this twilight zone of values in object-relations requires the utmost effort of both patient and analyst. Mere time and repetition will not accomplish the working through. This period, which usually covers at least two years of difficult work, can certainly be ranked with the task of the long-distance

* *See* Appendix E.

runner, mountain climber, and is often so represented in patient's dreams.

I believe that analysts practising in the Kleinian frame-work, which centres so much on character analysis and the achievement of integration, will not get through this difficult phase of the work with their patients without sustained "top performance". Without such clinical accomplishment their work will neither bear lasting fruit nor achieve conviction in their own minds. Patients not carried into the depressive position will relapse; scientific findings not bound, to some degree, to manifest and enduring clinical improvement in patients lose their anchorage in humanity and their supporting structure in social value. This may not render them less scientific nor correct, but will seem to their authors to rob them of importance. How long can a person endure in this strenuous work without the support of social accomplishment and scientific achievement? Not long, I think.

What, on the other hand, are the manifestations of the "damage" of which I speak, short of clinical breakdown? The answer is surprisingly simple and distressingly public. Failure of development! It must overtake almost every analyst eventually, for the vitality and concentration required for continued growth are not to be found except in the rare genius—a Freud, a Melanie Klein. Nor is it harmful to the movement for its tired members to fall back into conservative ranks, to become the modulators of exuberance. But it seems fairly clear that others who fall back from negligence or revulsion against the demands of the task become destructive critics and not modulators of progress.

APPENDICES

As explained in the Introduction, this book has grown in the milieu of lectures, seminars and supervisions, to some extent separated from the clinical work from which theoretical contributions to psycho-analytic literature derive. As a consequence a certain asynchrony is sometimes evident in the text in that reference is made to theoretical ideas which have not as yet taken their place in the literature.

In the following section these ideas and areas of development will be expanded, as a holding method, until future publications can give them more definition.

APPENDIX A—ACTING-OUT AND ACTING-IN THE TRANSFERENCE

These problems of analytic method and process are of special interest from the structural point of view and will be dealt with extensively by Dr. H. Rosenfeld in a future publication, which will carry forward the work begun in his paper, "An Investigation of the Need of Neurotic and Psychotic Patients to Act Out During Analysis."*

In the text I have referred to a particular aspect of acting-out of transference processes in children, of various ages and how these patterns of acting-out contribute form to their peer-relations and spontaneous group formation.

The latency child has a strong tendency to act-out his relations to internal parents and siblings, these latter also being parts of the self, by forming groups in which the pattern of family life and of adult social and political structure are mirrored. His clubs, secret societies and teams tend to be stable as regards roles, with more aggressive and imaginative children as leaders (parental functions) while weaker, more passive, younger or less intelligent children are dragooned into submission to the rules and procedures laid down

* In *Psychotic States*, Int. Psa. Library, No. 65, 1964.

(children functions). The obsessional tendency of this age group with its desexualisation of object relations through omnipotent control thus finds expression.

When puberty undercuts these obsessional defences by its genital upheaval, a very dramatic change is wrought in the basis of social life. This can be accurately studied in children who have been in analysis for some years during latency and are carried into puberty by means of a crisis of responsibility, as indicated in Chapter VI, shifting from playroom to adult consulting room and couch. In dreams and associations it becomes clear that a renewed splitting of the self and objects has occurred, requiring a reworking of infantile pregenital development in the light of the new genital desires and capacities. A particular pattern of acting-out tends to develop in puberty in which a group of four or five children, usually of one sex, will form a "delinquent" group, delinquent in its rebellious spirit though not necessarily in its outward behaviour. This group, in which the roles are constantly shifting, tends to reproduce the theme of excited, secret inquiry into the mystique of adult life. The roles are characteristically ones which might be labelled as, say, "fearless", "timid", "knowledgeable", "naive", "idealistic", "materialistic", etc.

These patterns of behaviour can be traced back to a particular type of masturbatory activity, prior to sleep, in which the fingers, personified, carry on excursions and skirmishes in the bed and on the body, employing its contours and orifices as the terrain of phantasy.

As puberty moves on to adolescence, the splitting alters and becomes more orderly again, dividing the infantile structures into more integrated segments, "good", "bad", "male", "female", with some distribution of intellect and passion.

The main point to be made is that the acting-out of the latency child is more object related, due to the massive externalisation of his internal relations, in keeping with his tendency to deny psychic reality. At puberty narcissism and splitting processes return in force and impose the new pattern, in which parts of the self are projected and the group is drawn together in a far more unstable but passionate way through the workings of mutual projective identification.

A preliminary communication on this subject is planned for the 1967 International Psycho-Analytical Congress by Mrs. E. Bick, while its special reference to autistic children is to be dealt with in a book by the author and a group of child analysts and psychotherapists who have carried out analysis under his supervision.

The thesis of these studies is that a very early failure of the child's experience of the "holding" function of the mother leaves a residual defect in basic integration of the self which manifests itself in a general weakness of integrative bonds at somatic levels of the self and a consequent fragility of experience of psychic reality. This gives rise to an excessive dependence on an external object to hold together the self in order that a sense of identity can be experienced. Separation causes a disintegration or falling to pieces, with incapacity for thought, disturbance in posture and motility, as well as vegetative disorganisation. This is seen by Mrs. Bick as related to failure of formation of the psychic equivalent of having a skin to hold the self together, a normal developmental product of identification with the adequate "containing" by the mother, both physical and psychological.

Primal object-self integration is a necessary preparation for the functioning of correct splitting-and-idealisation, as described by Melanie Klein. Failure to form this primal psychic skin may explain the tendency to loss of integration which is so severe in autism, where we find that introjection seems so severely impaired as to suggest that an internal world, a "space" within the self, cannot be conceived.

The problem of the "inside babies" has frequently been referred to in Melanie Klein's work and is beautifully illustrated in much of "Richard's" material in the early sessions of the "Narrative of a Child Analysis", especially in the undersea drawings with starfish-babies.

This conception of the inside of the mother's body appears to result from early experiences of omnipotent voyeurism (*see* p. 33 of my contribution to Adrian Stokes' *Painting and the*

Inner World, Tavistock, 1963). As such it is a consequence of envy and involves a sequence of phantasy which is an elaboration of envy of parental coitus as a part-object performance. The infant, dominated by his oral cravings, envisages the parental coitus as a banquet, to which the "inside-babies", but not "outside" ones, are invited.

While envy of parental objects is fraught with guilt, the "delusional jealousy" of the inside babies is sanctimoniously clung to with a sense of injustice which I have described in my paper "The Dual Basis of Materialism" to be published in "Forum of Psycho-analysis".

Another aspect of this area, of the relationship to the inside-babies is connected with terror, as a type of persecutory anxiety. It will be described in a paper to be read at the 1967 International Psycho-Analytical Congress. This paper ("Terror, Persecution and Dread—A Dissection of Paranoid Anxieties") will demonstrate that murderous masturbatory attacks on these internal babies produce persecutors, equivalent to ghosts, which inspire terror against which no defence can be mounted by the paralysed infantile self. It must turn for protection, either to good or bad objects. Turning to bad objects (or parts of the self in projective identification with external objects) is seen to play an important role in the genesis of addictions and perversions.

APPENDIX D—MUTILATIONS OF THE EGO

This is an example of one of the nosological categories with which we are attempting to construct a psycho-analytical classification. An interesting example of it can be found in the vivid description of the analysis of an adolescent suffering from near-fatal ulcerative colitis (H. S. Klein, "Notes on a case of ulcerative colitis" I.J.P.—46: 342: 1965.

It seems clear that a classification of disorders in childhood can only usefully be made on the basis of structural considerations, evidence for which can probably only accurately be collected in the course of psycho-analytical treatment.

APPENDIX E—HEALTH, STABILITY AND MATURITY

This is another reference to attempts being made to construct a psycho-analytical nosology. It follows to some extent the effort of Edward Glover (*J. of Ment. Sci.*—1932, 78: 819–842 but has a more specific reference to the psycho-analytical process, with psycho-genetic implications. The point of view involves no radical change but is more firmly connected with psychic structure and the relations of infantile structures to internal objects. Thus the overcoming of the use of massive projective identification as the principal mode of relations is viewed as the crucial step from mental illness to mental health, or the overcoming of psychosis. However, the concept of the establishment of the internal breast as the basis of *stability* in mental structure is implicit in Melanie Klein's work from early on and stands in connection with the emphasis she placed on masturbation phantasy as the instrument of regression.

The passing of the genital oedipus complex as the crucial step toward psycho-sexual maturity would not now be viewed as a task of which the small child could be capable, in line with the view that the latency period is primarily a holding position, relying more on obsessional mechanisms than repression itself for its stability. A fuller discussion of the differentiation between adult and infantile sexuality will be published* in which it will be shown how polymorphism in adult and infantile sexuality is based on identification and emulation, respectively, in regard to the polymorphous aspects of the coital relations of the internal parents. A clear distinction will be drawn between polymorphism and perversity, showing how the latter is related to inadequate splitting-and-idealisation, thus bringing together metapsychologically the perversions, addictions and psychopathies, somewhat in contrast to Freud's suggestion that perversions stand in close relation to the neuroses, as their converse.

APPENDIX F—OMNIPOTENCE AND OMNISCIENCE

The view is taken here that omnipotence is a quality of mind, linked to excitement, which must be differentiated from omniscience as an eipistemological theory which may be held by a part of the self. I hope to show how they are related in a

---

* "The Introjective Basis of Polymorphism in Adult Sexuality" read to the British Psycho-Analytical Society, 19th October, 1966.

paper "On Pornography"* in which I will discuss the functioning of omnipotence in the sensory realm and how it can produce a conviction of omniscience in certain parts of the infantile organisation. This omniscience has the meaning, "What I know is all there is to be known": this can be distinguished from the omniscience of primal objects, especially the mother's breast, which has the meaning of "containing all possible knowledge".

While this distinction views omnipotence as a quality of mind which must be generated, especially by masturbation, it does not see it as a defence in itself but only as an adjunct, a potentiator, of defensive operations, such as omnipotent control over objects. Again, to translate it into basic language, this excited state of mind would contain the attitude, "I can do it", whatever the "it" at issue may be, not "I can do everything". It is a transient state whipped up in relation to a task at hand. It may be unfortunate that it has come to be called *omnipotence*, but after all we cannot change our terminology every time a meaning requires refinement.

APPENDIX G—MODES OF MASTURBATION

The work of discriminating between different modes of masturbatory activity and their intrapsychic consequences is being carried forward by several investigators. In my paper on anal masturbation I have shown the relation of penetrating modes of masturbation to the operation of massive projective identification. In Appendix A a type of group acting-out in puberty was linked to a type of nocturnal masturbatory play in which the fingers are personified as parts of the self and objects. This is also linked with the tickling-touching-tapping type of activity mentioned in the text at this point, in connection with genitalisation. On the other hand the generating of omnipotence, mentioned in Appendix F, seems more related to the rubbing techniques, particularly of penis and clitoris and is therefore more related to manic consequences.

Mrs. Bick's paper mentioned in Appendix B on the role of the skin in personality organisation also deals with some of the perverse and sadistic autoerotisms, such as picking, scratching, and hair pulling.

* Read to the Imago Group, London—1966.

APPENDIX H—NARCISSISTIC ORGANISATION

Increased accuracy in identifying the splitting processes at infantile levels, both in adults and children, make it possible to speak with some conviction about the organisation of narcissism, just as Melanie Klein spoke of the organisation of object relations, and Karl Abraham described the organisation of the libido.

In a future paper, enlarging on his earlier study,* Herbert Rosenfeld plans to expand this theme, with the aim of divesting narcissism of its pre-psycho-analytic descriptive implication, giving it a definitive metapsychological meaning. It is felt that narcissistic organisations never, with the possible exception of the schizophrenic delusional system, exist entirely outside the sphere of objects. However, it proves to be of great clinical importance to be able to identify the locus of the organisation, especially whether it takes place inside or outside an object. For instance this proves to be of importance in the differentiation between psychopathic and addictive use of drugs, or between psychotic and neurotic types of antisocial acts.

APPENDIX I—THE PRIMACY OF PSYCHIC REALITY

Some reference to the ethical implications of psycho-analytical discoveries about the nature of the mental apparatus can be found in Roger Money-Kyrle's *Man's View of His World* (Duckworth, 1961) and in my dialogue with Adrian Stokes on the social structure of art in *Painting and the Inner World* (Tavistock, 1963). The primacy of psychic reality for human fulfilment is also dealt with in my paper, "A Return to the Imperative" (to be published).

The central theme of all these is that mental stability, self-esteem and satisfaction and therefore *Weltanschauung* in both perceptual and attitudinal aspects, are as Melanie Klein always stressed in the first instance a derivative of relations, at infantile levels, to primal good objects. Since introjective identification with these objects is the foundation upon which adult bisexuality must be based for its expansion, and since absolute determinist justice prevails in psychic reality, it can be claimed that, save for the workings of fate with its

* In *Psychotic States*—Int. Psa. Library, No. 65, 1964.

imponderable factors, the opportunity for completing the life cycle is open to all. The fact of "That's all there is", as Arnold Wesker stresses in his play *The Kitchen,* cannot reasonably be taken as a ground for pessimism or complaint. In contrast, psycho-analysis can confidently identify the infantile basis for the many claims for transcendental satisfactions.

APPENDIX J—HORIZONTAL AND VERTICAL SPLITTING

The "axes" of splitting processes are many, in respect both of self and objects. It seems almost certain that splitting of both self and object must proceed in parallel, in so far as splitting of the self necessarily involves perceptual capacities. Thus the perception of objects is immediately divided. When it is the object which is the primary locus of splitting, the cleavage probably tends immediately to impose a parallel split in the self, determined by the economics of object choice.

Splitting-and-idealisation appears in phantasy as a frontal splitting into right and left, from which the term "vertical" has been derived, to contrast it with divisions in the maturity levels of the self, akin to the layered, or "onion", structure of earlier analytic writing, which are called "horizontal".

However, "vertical" splitting may take many forms in the graphic sphere of unconscious phantasy. Top-bottom, front-back, inside-outside are well-known ramifications of the original right-left configuration in the division of good and bad in self and objects. In contrast to these modes, we find that the autistic child follows a mode of splitting of self and objects according to sensory modalities (see my paper "Autism, Schizophrenia and Psychotic Adjustment"—Acts of 2nd European Congress of Child Psychiatry—S. Harger, Rome), which would seem to be a prelude to the splitting between intellectual and emotional relationships characteristic of obsessional neurosis. This subject will be further discussed in a book of studies with autistic children, by the author and a group of collaborators.

APPENDIX K—DEATH-OF-THE-BREAST

As I have mentioned earlier in the text, time as a uni-directional, irreversible aspect of reality, cannot be fully apprehended until the various types of confusion have been resolved. Specifically, the disturbed time-orientation is as follows: (*a*) massive projective identification takes the patient's mental state into an area of phantasy-geography where time is non-existent; (*b*) the oscillation between remaining outside of primal objects and getting inside them has the effect of going back and forth between present and past, as can clearly be seen in dreams where one area of the dream is in the present while another may be, for instance, in the 18th century; (*c*) confusion between external reality and internal (psychic) reality carries with it a circular attitude about time, modelled on the traverse of the sun, in the manner of the ancient Egyptians who envisaged the ship of the sun being rowed through the underworld at night back to the Eastern horizon. A little girl said, "When the moon takes the sun away", indicating that the moon of the adults is seen by her as the ghost of the sun which has been taken away by an unseen object named "moon" (or "Mr. Moon", one suspects); (*d*) only at the threshold of the depressive position, when the penis-nipple comes to preside over the beauty and goodness of the white-part of the breast, as the primal combined object, does time become a dimension, and each moment becomes "lost" in the past, "used" or "wasted" in the present—and, above all, "hoped for" in the future.

These changes are most striking in the analysis of young children, thanks to their relative naïveté. The link between the analyst's watch, his eyes and the mother's nipples can be seen in the playroom to be unmistakably related to the father's penis, constantly suspected of cheating the child of time, like "Mr. Moon". This sense of grievance is particularly difficult for the child to overcome because of the concreteness with which the speed of passage of time seems to vary, fast in delight, slow in boredom, interminable in separation.

With this achievement of the sense of the reality of time in the outside world, the concept of a "life-time" arises, just as a concept of a "life-space" may be said to have arisen when the geographical confusions were resolved. The stage is set for the appreciation of death as an end of life-time, as distinct from all the more primitive forms of persecutory and blissful phantasies which had been given the name of "death".

Sparing, as a form of reparation, an extension of restitution, becomes possible—to spare the object the "time of its life".

APPENDIX L—TERMINOLOGY OF INTEGRATION

While research is still necessary to clarify the detailed processes of integration, Bion's investigations of the more minute significance of the shift from paranoid-schizoid to depressive position (Ps↔D) in the moment-to-moment economics of the mental apparatus makes it possible to define the terminology with some precision.

Integration—this is clearly a structural concept, standing in relation to *dis-integration* (not *splitting*, which is a dynamic concept) as *progression* stands to *regression* is the older topographic theories. It applies to objects, internal and external, as well as to the structure of the ego (or more correctly, the self). Integration of the self takes place in the sphere of the good objects, the various parts being drawn and bound together by their common loving attachment, in the first instance to the breast. Integration of objects comes about through the processes of reparation.

Reparation—this is a dynamic concept, governed by the economics of Ps↔D. In unconscious phantasy it is represented as a coital conjunction of part or whole-objects producing *combined objects*, in the first instance the penis-in-the-breast. By this means bad objects, whether produced by splitting-and-idealisation or by damaging masturbatory attacks (including projective identification) are restored and assimilated to the idealised objects.

Every increment of integration of objects intensifies the depressive pains of the good parts of the self, adult and infantile alike, since the richness and goodness of the objects are enhanced by integration. The governing economic principle is that this integration will proceed as far as the self will tolerate, in regard to the envy, jealous and depressive pain aroused. The dynamic terms referable to this tolerance are *sparing*, *restitution* and *responsibility*. The counterfeiting of these processes of toleration and reparation are covered by the terms *mock* and *manic* reparation.

Melanie Klein's work on these topics has been clearly summarised in Hanna Segal's *Introduction to the Work of Melanie*

Klein. Further developments are suggested in Bion's recent works, *Learning from Experience, The Elements of Psycho-analysis* and *Transformations.*

It is still uncertain whether the self can perform reparation to objects directly or only indirectly, through sparing, restitution and responsibility (for psychic reality). It is my view that they cannot, as can be seen from my discussion and material in the section on working through in Chapter VIII.

* Published by William Heinemann Medical Books Ltd, London.

INDEX

Abraham, K., 102
Acting-in, xv, 12, 62, 83, 96, 97
Acting-out, xv, 4, 5, 6, 12, 30, 34, 44, 62, 96, 97
Addiction, 31, 40
Adolescence, *see* Children
Adult, analysis, 53, 62
Adult part, xiii, xv, 38, 81
Anxiety, 7
    castration, 28
    claustrophobic, 16, 18, 19
    depressive, 86
    hypochondriacal, 19, 38
    modification, xii, 10, 86
    modulation, xii, xiii, 10, 86
    nameless dread, 16
    persecutory, 16
    relief, 6, 7
    separation, 2, 7, 9, 10, 14, 22, 30, 36, 37, 98
    terror, 16, 38
Attitude, 79, 84
Autism, 14, 15, 16, 17, 23, 98

Beauty, 28, 42, 45
Bick, E., 98, 101
Bion, W. R., 6, 21, 32, 50, 106
Breach of technique, *see* Technique
Break, *see* Separation

Castration, *see* Anxiety
Character, xiv, 4, 34
Child analysis, xv
Children,
    adolescent, 5, 22
    latency, 4, 8, 26, 53, 96
    pubertal, 8, 26, 53, 97
    young, 7, 26
Claustrophobia, *see* Anxiety
Clinical material, 17, 39, 42, 45, 47, 53–61, 63, 67, 77, 88–91, 104
Combined objects, 105
communication, ix, xii, xiv, 41

Confusion, viii
    geographical, 13, 20, 21, 22, 24
    good–bad, 14
    male–female, 40
    persecution–depression, 38
    time, 17, 43, 104
    zonal, 23, 25, 29, 30
Conscious, *see* Organ of Consciousness
Constitution, 10, 13
Container, xii
Contamination, 4, 10
Conviction, vii, xvi
Cooperation, 7, 11, 44, 60, 64
    pseudo, 7
Counter transference, xi, xii, 26, 81
Creation, xii, 94
Cure, xii, xiv
Cyclical time units, 14, 33, 76

Dead objects, 38
Death-of-the-breast, 47, 103
Defences, 9, 26
Dependence, 10, 25, 29, 33, 43, 46
Depressive position, xi, 39, 41, 86
    anxiety, *see* Anxiety
    threshhold of, 25, 31, 32, 39, 86
Differentiation, 4, 46
Discovery, xii, xiii
Dread, *see* anxiety
Dreams, 37, 38, 41, 44, 45
    "bath" dream, 55, 56
    classification, 64
    "climbing St. Paul" dream, 63, 64
    "friendly ape" dream, 55, 56, 59
    "girl behind the chest" dream, 57
    "head mistress" dream, 89
    "M. T. Brown" dream, 90
    "muddy lake and grassy bank" dream, 56, 60
    "ride in the car" dream, 90
    "sample of jealousy" dream, 59, 60, 87

Dreams (*contd.*)
  "sewer" dream, 56, 62
  "white chest" dream, 57

Economics, 13, 26, 31, 43
Envy, 15
Erikson, E. H., 24
Evolution of the transference, xvi, 8
Excitement, 27
Externalisation, 4, 5, 34

Father's-penis, 30, 32, 40
Feeding-breast, 30, 32
Folie à Deux, 3, 6, 31, 85
Freud, Sigmund, 7, 24, 33, 81, 85, 86, 92, 93, 95

Gathering of the transference, xvi, 3, 7, 9, 12
Geographical confusion, *see* Confusion
Geography, viii, xvi
Glover, E., 100

Holiday, *see* Separation
Hypochondria, *see* Anxiety

Identification, 4
  see Projective
  with persecutor, 18
Identity, 21
Impasse, *see* Resistance–Intractable
Inside-baby, 18, 24, 30, 40, 99
Inside-penises, 40
Insight, xii
Integration, 39, 44, 46, 48, 49, 105
Internal objects, 8
  equipment of, 88, 91
Interpretation, xii, 3, 6, 10, 78, 83, 87
Interruption, xiii, xiv, 46, 50, 51
Introjection, 2, 6, 20, 25, 33, 88
  identification, 38, 86

Jaques, Elliott, 11
Jealousy, 15, 25, 28
  delusion of, 15
  delusional, 15, 98
  possessive, 15, 39
Jones, E., 27
Joseph, Betty, 15

Klein, H. S., 99

Klein, Melanie, vii, xi, 3, 6, 15, 16, 21, 26, 49, 85, 95, 98, 100, 102, 105

Latency, *see* Children

Masturbation, 24, 27, 36, 38, 48, 97, 101
Maturity, 99
Mental health, 22, 23, 99
Method, xiv, 3, 92
Modification of anxiety, *see* Anxiety
Modulation of anxiety, *see* Anxiety
Money-Kyrle, R., 102
Mutilation of the ego, 18, 99
Mutual idealisation, 27, 30

Nameless dread, *see* Anxiety
Narcissism, 5, 6, 28, 29, 30, 31, 34, 35, 102
Natural history, xiv, 3, 10, 12, 50, 78
Nosology, xiv, xv, 99
Notation, viii, 50

Object relation, 4
  see, Container, Combined objects, Dead object, Father's-penis, Feeding-breast, Inside-baby, Inside-penis, Internal objects, Penis-in-the-breast, Toilet-breast
Obsessional mechanism, 26
  see Omnipotent control, Denial of psychic reality
Oedipus complex, 24, 25, 27, 32, 39, 40, 48
Omnipotence, 9, 10, 37, 40, 86, 100
  control, 10, 18, 19, 26, 38, 84
Omniscience, 15, 40, 100
Organ of consciousness, xii, xiii, 62
Organisation, xiii

Paranoid-schizoid position, xi
Penis-in-the-breast, 39, 105
Persecution, *see* Anxiety
Possession, 27, 28, 42
Preside, xii, 13, 45
Primary rule, 11
Prognosis, xiv, xv
Progress, xiv, 49
Projective identification, xi, 6, 16, 19, 25, 28, 42, 86, 87
  Massive, 9, 13, 15, 16, 17, 18, 20, 21, 22, 23, 25
Pseudo—maturity, 21, 38

Pseudo (*contd.*)
—analysis, 42, 44
—cooperation, *see* Cooperation
—transference, *see* Transference
Psychic reality, 4, 28, 34, 36, 37, 38, 39, 44, 47, 62, 102
denial of, 20
Psychoanalytical process, *see* Natural history
Puberty, *see* Children

Regression, 19
Relief, *see* Anxiety
Reparation, 30, 31, 41, 42, 48, 105
manic, 42, 105
Reproduction, 48
Resistance, 5
intractable, 22, 31, 43, 50, 52
Responsibility, 37, 39, 46, 105
Rhythm, 7, 10, 41
Rosenfeld, H., 96, 102
Russell, Bertrand, xi

Segal, Hanna, viii, 105
Self-analysis, xiii, 39, 46
Separation anxiety, *see* Anxiety
Setting, xii, xiv, 3, 6, 8, 9, 19, 42, 52, 78
Skin—psychic equivalent of, 14, 98
as a zone, 27
Somatic delusions, 38
Splitting, xiii, 4, 39, 49, 88
of levels,
Horizontal, xiii, 4, 21, 37, 103
vertical, xii, 4, 103
of objects, 20
of self, 38, 49
Stability, xiii, 99
Stokes, Adrian, 98

Structure, xi, xiii
Style, xiii, 79
Supervision, 66
Symptoms, 4, 5

Technique, 8, 19, 37, 42, 49, 52, 53, 79
breach of, 19, 42
Termination, xiii, 39, 44, 46, 50
premature, 48
see Interruption
Terminology, viii
Terror, *see* Anxiety
Toilet-breast, 20, 21, 23, 24, 25, 32
Transference, xi, xiv, xv, 6, 7
cure, 7
deepening of, 9, 10
pre-formed, 7
pseudo, 7
resolution, 47
shift of, 67
Traumatic factors, 52
Trust, 15, 33, 35, 37, 40, 42

Unconscious, xii

Validation, xvi
Virtuosity, xvi, 93
Voyeurism, 40
see Omniscience

Week-end, *see* Separation
Weening, 41, 44, 47
Wesker, A., 103
Work, xii, 60, 79, 80, 82, 83
Working through, 10, 13, 14, 78, 82, 85, 91

Young children, *see* Children